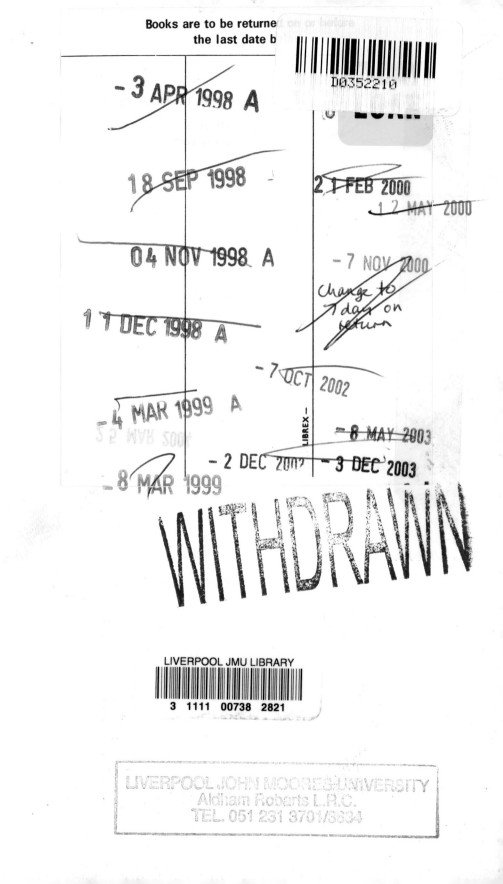

The Parental Obligation:
A Study of Parenthood Across Households

MAVIS MACLEAN and JOHN EEKELAAR

·HART·
PUBLISHING

OXFORD
1997

Hart Publishing
Oxford
UK

Distributed in North America by
Northwestern University Press
625 Colfax, Evanston IL
60208-4210 USA

Hart Publishing is a specialist legal publisher based in Oxford, England.
To order further copies of this book or to request a list of other
publications please write to:

Hart Publishing, 19 Whitehouse Road, Oxford, OX1 4PA
Telephone: +44 (0)1865 434459 or Fax: (0)1865 794882 or 434459
email Hartpub@janep.demon.co.uk

British Library Cataloguing in Publication Data
Data Available
ISBN 1–901362–22–1 (hardback)
1–901362–23–X (paperback)

Typeset in 10pt Sabon
by SetAll, Abingdon
Printed in Great Britain on acid-free paper
by Biddles Ltd. Guildford and Kings Lynn

This book is dedicated to the memory of our fathers
Alexander Linning
Jan (John) Eekelaar

Contents

Acknowledgements

The findings reported in this book were the result of research funded by the Economic and Social Research Council, Grant No. R.000234433. We record our thanks to the Council for this funding. Sarah Beinart, of Social and Community Planning Research (SCPR), gave us invaluable help in developing the project, organizing the fieldwork and contributing to the analysis; Dymphna Hermans gave us helpful advice on statistical matters and Lynda Clarke kindly read the text in draft. We are particularly grateful to them, but we also derived much assistance from conversations with colleagues, especially Gwyn Davis, Martin Richards and Carol Smart. As always, we are grateful to Jenny Dix of the Centre for Socio-Legal Studies, Oxford, for her administrative help.

Mavis Maclean
John Eekelaar
Oxford

29 April 1997

1

The Themes of the Study

OBLIGATIONS AND PARENTHOOD

Obligations are what we ought to do. They provide reasons for acting in certain ways. But where they come from is not always easy to tell. Most people surely think that parents have obligations towards their children. What kind of obligations are these? There must be moral obligations, but morality requires us to respect everybody, not just our children. Perhaps morality requires us to do more for our children than for other people and even other people's children. But if a couple bring up someone else's child, does not morality require them to support and care for that child as if the child was their own? Perhaps, therefore, any moral obligations you have towards your children which you do not have regarding other children arise from the fact that you are bringing them up in your household rather than because they are your own children. Are you then perhaps morally obliged to bring up your children? If that were so, arranging adoption or long-term fostering of your children would be immoral.[1]

While moral principles to care for others and promote human flourishing must underpin all our obligations towards all children, those principles are, as Tony Honoré (1993) has observed, "incomplete" guides to conduct because they do not always indicate who owes which obligations to whom, when, and to what extent. The general exhortation to care for others needs institutional arrangements (such as taxation or public health services) to be effective. Hence many moral principles are given substance through social and legal mechanisms. The same is true of obligations towards children. The central concerns of this study are about the way in which parenthood in itself acts as a mediating mechanism through which these background moral principles are converted into legal and social obligations and to examine the structure of these obligations, including apparent conflicts between them.

This is not so easy to discover while parents and children are living together. As we will explain in Chapter 3, when members of a family are living together, the law is strangely reticent in articulating and enforcing the obligations they may owe to one another. That does not mean that they do not have duties to each other. But these duties may be only indirectly

---

[1] See Eekelaar (1991) arguing that a rule requiring that children be cared for by their natural parents is a contingent and not a necessary instantiation of a moral duty to promote human flourishing.

recognized or enforced by the law. Indeed, they may not be legal duties at all. A complete account of family obligations must include social as well as legal obligations and indicate the interaction between them. This will be discussed in detail in Chapter 3, but this chapter will include a consideration of the conceptual distinctions between them (pp. 4–8 below).

PATHWAYS THROUGH CHILDHOOD

This is, however, not only a conceptual study but also an empirical one. In order to understand more about the parental obligation, we decided to obtain more information about how parents dealt with one another on matters which affected their children. But we did not look at parents who were living together. This is partly because it is difficult to disentangle and articulate the variety of obligations between family members who are living together. But it is also because this is a socio-legal study, and we are particularly interested in the implications of people's behaviour for legal policy. The American socio-legal theorist Donald Black (1989: 11) claimed that the law tends to be less implicated in people's dealings the closer they are related to each other and that the greater the social distance is between people, the more likely it is that the law will enter into their relationship. It may be more accurate to say that when family relationships are combined with close social distance (for example, sharing a household) legal regulation is less likely than where people live at a distance, even though they have a family relationship. People who live together may have differences, but these enmesh with the dynamic of the entire relationship, and can frequently be resolved within that dynamic. So quarrels or misunderstandings can often be resolved in the context of the general benefits which sharing a household holds for each partner. Resorting to law has negative implications which outweigh the benefits of the interactive relationship. But if people live apart, a point of tension or dispute can become the dominant focus of the relationship; there may be few, if any, compensating benefits which are threatened by legal intervention. It therefore becomes necessary to define more sharply what their legal obligations are and to provide mechanisms for regulating them. Or so one may suppose. One purpose of our study was to see how far empirical evidence was consistent with such a supposition.

We therefore wished to contact parents who lived apart, and we did so through a survey of the general population which screened out our respondents by asking the question: "Are you the natural or adoptive parent of a child under eighteen whose other parent lives elsewhere?". (The design and methodology of the study is described on pp. 153–8 below). This question both selects those cases where legal involvement (and therefore the relevance of legal obligations) is most significant and also those where the defining relationship between the parties is that of *common parenthood*. It includes parents who have never lived together, parents who lived together without being married but who are now living apart, parents who are divorced, parents who are still living alone and cases where either or both parents have re-partnered in some way. The only thing they have in common is that they were not, at the time of interview, bringing up the child in a common household.

This data set corresponds to none of the standard models. These are usually defined exclusively in terms of the parents' relationship to one another: never-married, cohabitants (or former cohabitants), once-married but now divorced or separated, one-parent families, stepfamilies and reconstituted families. These terms have developed to reflect the growing complexity of family groupings, but they have a static air about them, perhaps suggesting the groupings are more fixed than they are. As we examined our data we felt it would be more helpful to develop a more organic categorization, more closely grounded in the child's experience. The children in our study could have originated in any of these groupings. They also may have passed through a number of them. By closely analysing the pathways followed by the children, we hoped to be able to throw light on the implications for the parental relationship (and therefore for the parental obligation) of the family and household circumstances into which the child was born and the events subsequent to that. In order to reduce analysis to practicable proportions, where households reported more than one child, we randomly selected one child whose pathway was tracked. This we call the "study" child.

It will be evident that the data revealed an immensely complex scene of changing family constellations. However, in the exposition of the data we have chosen to divide our children into three main groups based on the family circumstances into which they were born. We start (Chapter 5) with children who had *never* lived together with *both* their biological parents at the same time. Since the two-parent family remains the ideological norm, it seemed important to track the family histories of children who had never received joint parenting in the same household by their natural parents. These children therefore were born to parents who were neither married to one another nor living together either when the child was born or at time of the interview. The group comprises children born to women living alone at the time of the birth and those born to women living with another adult (a husband or cohabitant who was not the child's father) or adults (usually her parents). There was even a small number, hitherto unrecognized in conventional analysis, where the child was born to a mother who was living alone and apart from the father after having divorced him. We have not found a simple expression to describe this category, for we are trying to overcome the failure of static terms like "one-parent family" and "stepfamily" to reveal that many children who do not spend their childhood with both biological parents pass *through* these situations and others, and to do so by focusing on the relationships which the child has rather than those of the adults.

Since they comprise all the children not falling into the first group, the remaining two groups of children would have all shared a home with both their parents when they were born, but were no longer living with both parents. They might now be living with only one adult, or in a reconstituted two-adult household. We have divided these according to whether their parents were or were not married to each other at the time of the child's birth. The reason for doing this is that, historically, the obligations of parenthood have been closely linked to the marital status of the parents. As will be explained in Chapter 3, this connection has been greatly reduced in recent years. Nevertheless, the significance and role of marriage is now much discussed, and the behaviour of couples who live together without marriage is imperfectly understood. It seemed important, therefore, to see what differences there might be in parent-child relationships across households between cases where the formerly cohabiting parents were married and those where they were not. Our findings are discussed in Chapters 6 and 7.

OBLIGATIONS AND BEHAVIOUR

For the most part our data describe the shifting dealings and inter-relationships which occur between parents and children, and between parents, when a united household breaks up, or fails to emerge. Yet this claims to be a book about the parental obligation, and "obligation" carries with it some notion of rules. What, it may be asked, can be said about rules on the basis only of descriptions of what people do? Surely it is necessary to know why they acted as they did. Yet we did not ask our respondents about their motivations. Our reason was that a person's motivations for doing an act are analytically independent from whether the person was (or should have been) under an obligation to do the act. This position requires justification, and that in turn requires a distinction to be drawn between legal and social obligations. This is also important because the former have the indorsement of the state and are therefore more formidable than social rules, although by the same token they are susceptible to the mechanisms of legal process and change and may therefore be less embedded in society than some social rules.

The nature of legal obligations

Legal philosophers and social scientists have given much thought to how legal and social obligations might be distinguished. This is not so easy as one might think, because some people have urged that the "true" law may not necessarily be found in law books, but by looking at the practices people "actually" follow; what is sometimes said to be the "living law". But then it might be difficult to know what the difference is between legal obligations and the obligations imposed by morality or even social convention. So it seems that we must distinguish between obligations which have their source in some institution and those which do not.[2] Theories of law which are often called "positivist" typically *assume* the presence of state agencies and explain law as being in some way related to, or proceeding from, those agencies.[3] Obligations are "legal" obligations, therefore, if they derive from institutions which are accepted by other agencies, or by themselves, as sources of legal obligation. This may seem to be circular, and indeed it is. "Law", in this positivist sense, is essentially a self-defining concept: its existence is dependent on the presence of institutions recognized as law-creating or law-observing.

But even authoritatively enacted law requires interpretation. Suppose a judge interprets a law in a way we believe to be wrong. Can we say we believe the decision to be wrong and yet that it creates a legal obligation?[4] The answer is both yes and no, depending on which of two distinguishable, but equally proper, perspectives of law is being used. One is descriptive from the social scientific viewpoint; it addresses the nature of obligations which bind the citizen. The other is normative; it examines the process of the formation and application of the law. Although a judge who looks up the law in a book when deciding a case and a citizen who consults the same book when seeking information about his obligations, seem to be equally "bound" by the law they read there, their positions are very different. Citizens are expected to obey the law; judges (acting judicially) are expected to apply it. The citizen and his legal adviser may well "interpret" what they read, but the way a citizen interprets the law, whether or not he obeys it, and his motives for action,[5] have no consequence for the existence or content of the law. What makes a decision "law" for the citizen is that a "decisive moment"[6] defined by the institutional structure as conferring legal status upon it has occurred. Hence for the citizen the social forces which influence that decision (such as the personality of the judge, the ethnicity of the jury[7]) form a legitimate part of the citizen's experience and understanding of the law.

But a judge's role is integral to the institution of law; her application, or refusal to apply, a law has every consequence for the existence and content of law because it is ultimately through the judge that the law finds its expression. For the judge, the law is what she interprets it to be and she cannot (if she acts properly) take into account the non-interpretive (or predictive)

---

[2] For an account of the importance of state institutions in western concepts of "law", and the contrast with attempts by some social scientists to treat social practice as "law", see Tamanaha (1995).

[3] These theories are elaborated in the standard works on legal theory.

[4] This puzzle has been at the root of a dispute between "interpretivist" and "positivist" theorists. It is well captured in Hart (1994: Postscript).

[5] Hence Hart has said that the motives a citizen may have for following a rule are immaterial as to the rule's existence: Hart (1994: 115).

[6] See Raz (1996: 13).

[7] These are the many features which, according to Donald Black (1989), form part of "sociological jurisprudence".

elements that form part of the citizen's experience of the law.[8] So it is not inconsistent to accept that a judge engaged in applying the law, or some other participant engaged in the legal process, must hold that a wrong interpretation creates no legal obligation and also that a social scientist can describe the same interpretation as representing "the law".

So from the citizen's, and the social scientist's, point of view, we can identify legal obligations as those which derive from institutionally authoritative sources, whether we agree with the interpretations they represent or not, and whatever motives people have for following, or not following, them. But we need to make some further preliminary distinctions relevant to the context of family obligations. We can separate *direct* from *indirect* legal obligations. A law which says that a husband must support his wife and provides the wife with a remedy to enforce the obligation, imposes a direct obligation. But if the law gives no remedy to the wife, but merely allows the state to recover a contribution from the husband towards any benefits it sees fit to provide as a result of his failure to support her, the husband's obligation is enforced indirectly. Since the extent to which his obligation is enforced, if at all, depends on persons other than his wife, it can be said to be an indirect obligation.

Social obligations

This analysis can be taken further. Suppose that the government withholds social benefits from 16-year-old children, or ceases financing their educational aspirations, in the expectation that family members will "feel obliged" to provide the money instead. Is the government incorporating that sense of obligation into the "law"? The government may wish to encourage, or discourage, acts which are not legally required but which people may be disposed to do.

We may think of these acts as obligations, but if they do not arise directly from an institutional source, they are social and not legal obligations. But how do we know when social obligations exist? It is, it seems, very difficult to identify social rules. As Hart (1994: 50–60) has famously observed, we cannot simply observe regularities in behaviour and assume that there is a rule that people should behave in that way. That would make the mistake of deriving an "ought" from an "is". According to Hart, people act on rules if group members have accepted that "the general conformity of a group to (rules) is part of the reasons which its individual members have for acceptance" (1994: 255). There should be "consensus of convention". Perhaps, then, we could ask people why they act in certain ways and whether one reason is that they "feel" they "ought" to do what they do? But Janet Finch (1989: 146) has pointed out that "the matter is quite complex because one of the grounds upon which

---

[8] Hence Hart writes that, unlike the citizen, the judge cannot have a "merely personal concern" with rules; for the judge, rules *must* be regarded from the "internal point of view" as representing the appropriate standards of behaviour: Hart (1994: 115–6).

people justify their own actions is that they are only doing (or not doing) the same as most other people". Does this mean they are doing it because everyone does it, or because they think everyone *ought* to do it? Even if they think everyone ought to do it, is this because it is a tenet of their personal morality, perhaps shared by few others, or because they believe (rightly or wrongly?) that most people also feel it should be done? These matters are hard enough to grasp conceptually, and Finch has explained how difficult it is to ascertain empirically whether, in familial relations, a person's actions towards another were grounded, even partially, in the belief that "there is a social rule" requiring those actions. They may have no clear idea what the "socially approved" position is, or think there is such a position when this is unlikely, or act because "that's the way the world is" rather than on a normative belief.

For these reasons we believed it would have unnecessarily complicated and extended our (already long) interviews by seeking to discover the motivations for people's specific actions. This would have been wrong had we intended to explain our respondents' actions and to contribute towards a theoretical understanding of social action. As W.G. Runciman (1983: 15) observed, the social sciences seek to explain human behaviour through understanding it, and in this context the concept of understanding must be broken down into "its primary, secondary and tertiary senses". The first sense is understanding what is necessary for the reportage of what occurs; the second is understanding how it came about; and the third is understanding what the actions meant from the point of view of the actor (the hermeneutic or *verstehende* approach).

But we are not intent on "explaining" or "understanding" parents' behaviour. This is not a sociological study in that sense. It is an account of parental behaviour in the context of legal and social policy. We can demonstrate parents' legal obligations from the content of the law. We do not need to prove the "existence" of social obligations by an elaborate construction of the nature of the reasons, or partial reasons, some of the parents might say that they had for their actions. It is enough if we can show that the structure of the law and legal policy itself *assumes* the existence of social rules. While of course mere regularities of behaviour do not establish their existence, they may provide grounds for making (or rejecting) that assumption. Rules reflect values and therefore the policy-makers will be inclined to assume that behaviour patterns they consider desirable are based on social rules or, if not, that they should be. For example, there may be no legal obligation for absent parents to maintain contact with their children. Yet if the policy-maker considers this desirable, absent parents may be treated as if they ought to keep contact; as if that were a social obligation.

For the reasons given above, our data cannot directly demonstrate whether or not there actually *is* a social obligation in such circumstances. But they can help in two ways. Law is a purposive activity, and policy-makers seek results. By examining people's actual behaviour, we can make more visible the terrain upon which the policy-makers' laws and assumptions operate. Are their assumptions consistent with people's behaviour? Even more, we could discover whether the respondents shared these assumptions. We did this by seeking their opinions about what should be done in certain archetypal fact-situations which we consider significant to the content of the parental obligation. Our respondents' views may not correspond to popular opinion, nor do they necessarily reflect their own motivations for action. But they do indicate the assumptions which people who have direct experience of some of the circumstances under consideration make about the social obligations which they think do, or should, prevail in those conditions.

DÉMARIAGE: THE COLLAPSE OF A LEGAL ORDER

We conclude this introductory chapter by placing our work within a general historical context. As we have observed above, our concern is with the obligations to which parenthood, in and of itself, may give rise. The reason for choosing this perspective arises from the apparent legal revolution caused by the collapse of marriage as the central organising institution of legal, familial relationships.

This is at first sight a startling statement. But when we refer to the collapse of marriage, we do not refer to any changes which may have occurred in the popularity or stability of marriage (which will be considered in Chapter 2), but to its status as a legal institution. The distinguished French legal sociologist, Irene Théry (1993), has described the era which began slowly to emerge after the 1960s as that of *démariage*. There is no English equivalent for this term. Théry uses it in a special way. It captures the intense social change from a time when marriage symbolized society's highest ideals to the present, when marriage has become a private matter, a subjective experience, to be entered, or left, as a matter of individual choice (Théry (1993: 13–14)). *Démariage* represents the significant disengagement of the institution of marriage, including the effects of its dissolution, from institutional social structures. *Démariage* has no necessary relationship to the number of people who marry (although it may affect this indirectly). It is, however, directly related to the *frequency* with which individuals marry, because the withdrawal of institutional regulation over entry to and, especially, exit from marriage opens the way for individuals to move more easily into and out of what is becoming an essentially private arrangement.

But, Théry observes, this disengagement from *marriage* does not imply the abandonment of institutional involvement in *family structures*. Indeed, it may promote its increase. She gives the example of what she takes to be the goal of mediation, namely, that despite the dissolution of marriage through divorce the *family* survives.[9] This took legislative expression in France with the law

---

[9] Théry (1993: 327–30).

of 8 January 1993 which was founded on the principle that, even after a divorce, parents should still raise their children *together*. If the couple had not married, the same principle applied, but only if they recognized their joint parenthood *while living together*: the family, once constituted by cohabitation, survives its dissolution.[10]

Anglo-American family lawyers have observed the decline in the legal importance of marriage for some years. In 1976 Mary Ann Glendon (1976) surveyed legal developments in the USA which, she prophesied, foreshadowed "the withering away of marriage". The state had significantly reduced its supervision over entry into marriage (making marriage more a matter of free individual choice) while at the same time reducing the distinctions between the legal consequences of marrying and of living together outside marriage. She referred to cases where custody issues were determined in much the same way where the parents had not married as they would be if they had been married (1976: 689). In public law, she noted that dependency, not legitimacy, was becoming the basis of entitlement to state benefits derived through parents. She concluded that, while it was unlikely that the benefits attaching to the married state would disappear overnight, "although the legal forms remain, social and economic developments are emptying them of some of their content" (1976: 710).

Glendon returned to this theme in her major comparative review of family law in the USA and Western Europe (Glendon, 1989). Here Glendon emphasized the withdrawal of state regulation over many areas of family life and the "pervasive" tendency for law and social programmes "to break the family down into its component parts and treat family members as separate and independent" (1989: 295). She perceived a "relaxation of family support ties" and, although accepting that child support was everywhere still recognized as an obligation of both parents, remarked that "contributions from absent fathers play a decreasing role—relative to public assistance and the mother's earnings—in the support of female-headed families" (1989: 296). This was all taking place within a context in which modern family law was relinquishing "most of its overt attempts to promote any particular set of ideas about family life" (1989: 297). Instead, it seemed that the state was coming into increased contact with individuals, dispensing with mediating groups, such as the family (1989: 298–306).

We have argued elsewhere (Eekelaar and Maclean (1994: 16–17)) that the legal watershed precipitating this change in England and Wales was the advent of no-fault divorce in 1971.[11] Prior to 1971, marriage was *in principle*

---

[10] Théry (1993: 331–3).

[11] The reformed divorce system enacted in the Family Law Act 1996 has been represented as if it introduced no-fault divorce for the first time. This is inaccurate. The 1971 reform established "irretrievable breakdown" as the sole ground for divorce. If divorce was required quickly, it was necessary to make *allegations* of fault, but these were never investigated and difficult to defend if made. The 1996 Act simply brought the reality underlying the 1971 system into the open.

a life-long commitment, or at least a commitment defeasible only in defined circumstances which were subject to external (judicial) supervision. It followed, therefore, that if the marriage was permitted to be dissolved, conditions could be imposed upon either party which created obligations for the period following the termination of the marriage. Under no-fault divorce, however, either partner may, *in principle*, bring the marriage to an end whenever he or she (privately) determines this should happen. In these circumstances it becomes less easy to use the event of the termination of marriage as an occasion to impose further obligations on either spouse, at least if these obligations are grounded only on the fact of the parties' marriage, because this might restrict freedom to divorce.

This generated deep uncertainties over what marriage was supposed to mean. If it was no longer a life-long commitment, what was it? The crisis was rendered all the more serious by the fact that the introduction of no-fault divorce coincided with the culmination of a long process by which legal reform and the availability of legal aid allowed divorce to spread from a privileged sector of the population to the whole population. So the moment when no-fault divorce virtually removed the prescriptive content from marriage law, it did so for *everyone*. The legal emptiness of marriage created a void that needed to be filled if family obligations were to survive. Some had already begun to address the question. In 1980, in a visionary paper, Eric Clive (1980), who later became a Scottish Law Commissioner, analysed the legal components of marriage and asked the challenging question whether most of these could be achieved by various legal means independent of the institution of marriage itself, and Brenda Hoggett (1980), who subsequently became a member of the English Law Commission, wrote that "we should be considering whether the legal institution of marriage continues to serve any useful purpose".

When Glendon observed and described the big picture, where the familial obligations of one adult towards another deriving from its traditional basis, marriage, were seen to have been dramatically weakened, it might have been difficult to discern the potential strength of any newly-emerging alternative ground for the derivation of familial obligations. In the mid-1990s, this new model has become clearer. John Dewar (1992: 52–3) has remarked that "cohabitation, and especially parenthood, are becoming more important as the determinants of legal status of family members, outgrowing marriage in importance in this respect". The increasing emphasis on the significance of parenthood is illustrated by the appearance of an excellent legal text on the law of parenthood: Barton and Douglas (1995). As we will explain in Chapter 3, there are indeed good reasons for thinking that parenthood is emerging as a new model for the source of family obligations, and it is a major purpose of this study to examine this closely.

It might be thought that the enactment of the Family Law Act 1996, and the debate which accompanied it, indicates an attempt to reverse the trends discussed above and re-assert the legal significance of marriage. This Act introduced a procedure which, when put in place, will allow divorce only after a period of "consideration and reflection"[12] has passed after one or both of the parties have lodged a statement declaring that the marriage has broken down. Many of the Act's supporters believed that this mechanism will support marriage, while its opponents believed it would undermine it further. In fact, it is likely to make little difference to the drift of marriage into the private domain. It has not changed the significance (or insignificance) of marriage to the legal and (assumed) social obligations of people who marry and who do not marry. Indeed, it strongly encourages the *private* settlement between married people (especially through mediation) of their legal and social obligations. At most, the procedural obstacles to divorce, in particular, the delay, can be viewed as an attempt to encourage, or create, for married people, a *social* obligation to live together for life which the legislators think they have, or ought to have, the *legal* obligation having been removed.

There therefore seem good reasons to accept Théry's thesis about *démariage*. But even if we do this, and note the increasing *legal* significance of parenthood over marriage, it remains important to see how far marriage might affect the exercise of parenthood. Marriage may be becoming de-institutionalized, but it remains a significant personal context in which parenthood is initiated and implemented. One of the main objects of this study was to find out more about the role marriage had to play in the complex of relationships centred on parenthood.

---

[12] This is, for childless couples, at least nine months; where there are dependent children or one party requests it, the period is at least fifteen months. In all cases, an additional three months must also have passed after the initiating party or parties has attended an "information meeting": Family Law Act 1996, ss. 7(3), (6), (13), 8(2).

2

The Social Context

We referred in the previous chapter to the significance as far as legal regulation is concerned of where family members live in relation to one another.
This also has important economic consequences. It is obviously cheaper for
people to live together in one household than in separate households. In this
chapter we will explain, first, how the map of people's living arrangements
has changed during the course of this century. This presents an essentially static picture of the living arrangements of family members at any one time. The
picture, however, is one with which, we would argue, social policy has not
yet come completely to terms. We will then look at the changes that have
occurred over this period to the dynamics of individuals' family living
arrangements; that is, the way these arrangements change for individuals over
the course of their lives. This information, taken together, will help to clarify
the dilemmas facing social and legal policy with respect to people who are living separately from one another.

HOUSEHOLDS

Fragmentation of households: more people living alone

The structure of a household changes as a family progresses through its life
cycle. Nevertheless, historical and demographic evidence can disclose broad
pictures of how households are standardly constituted. The first lesson the evidence teaches is that there has been no point in recent British history where
co-residence by the extended family has been common. At no period of historical relevance to the present day have three generations of family members
commonly lived together. From as long ago as the mid-seventeenth century,
only about 5 to 7 per cent of households contained members of three generations.[1] In 1970, 4 per cent of people living in households were relatives (other
than the spouse or child) of the household head, just the same as in the period
1650–1749.[2] It seems never to have been common for a newly married couple
to live with their parents-in-law.[3] However, the mean *size* of the British house-

---

[1] Coleman and Salt (1992: 14); Haskey (1996c).
[2] Coleman and Salt (1992: 223).
[3] Macfarlane (1986: 92–8).

hold was about 4.6 for many centuries, until it started to decline in the 1920s.[4] The decline from that number to 2.44 in 1994[5] therefore marks one of the major changes which have occurred this century in the way we live. But the decline was not caused by pushing grandparents, in-laws or siblings out of the household. The reasons were the decline in the number of births in the family (although this was countered somewhat by decreasing mortality) and the departure of non-family members, like servants and lodgers. Households are therefore now standardly *smaller* than they used to be.

But households are not only smaller than before. Over the course of this century there has been a significant increase in the proportion of people *living alone*. Single-*person* (not single-*parent*) households were 5 per cent of all households in 1911; in 1994 the proportion was 27 per cent.[6] As stated earlier, this is not because of a decline in three-generation households, but is a result of changes in life expectancy, fertility and marriage patterns. In the past, a woman might have borne her last child when she was about forty. Even if the child left the home when in its late teens (as may have been common), once the last child left, the parents would not expect to live much longer.

Although, as we will see, women are now postponing child-bearing to a later age than in the immediate post-war period, this is within a context of sharply decreased fertility (see p. 17 below). The main increase in single-person families is therefore among the elderly whose children have long left home. The proportion of people over 65 in Great Britain rose from 10.9 per cent in 1951 to 15.6 per cent in 1987, and is expected to reach 19.2 per cent in 2027.[7] The proportion of *households* occupied by one person over retirement age rose from 7 per cent in 1961 to 16 per cent in 1994.[8] Increases are also to be found in the younger population. In 1973, 2 per cent of the population in Great Britain aged between 25 and 44 lived alone; in 1994 this had risen to 8 per cent. The number of women who live alone increases sharply after they reach 45. The majority of these people (especially the men) have never been married.[9] In fact, the *proportion* of households comprising an adult couple with dependent children decreased from 38 per cent in 1961 to 25 per cent in 1994. A greater proportion of households consists of just one person (28 per cent in 1994); but a still greater proportion (33 per cent) consists of an adult couple without dependent children.[10]

---

[4] Laslett (1983: 96, Table 7).

[5] *General Household Survey 1994* (OPCS, 1996), 15.

[6] Utting (1995: 11). *General Household Survey 1994*, 23. The proportion has stabilized over the past two years.

[7] Kiernan and Wicks (1990: 22).

[8] Kiernan and Wicks (1990: 19). *General Household Survey 1994*, 245. This proportion dropped slightly from 17% in the previous year.

[9] See Haskey (1987).

[10] *General Household Survey 1994*, 25.

Households consisting of families headed by one parent

The growth in the number of one-*parent* families is only one facet of this general trend. It raises particularly difficult issues, however, because of the complexity of the expectations held both by the individuals concerned and by society generally about what the relationship between the parents (if both are alive) should be. The increase in these families has been sharp (from 2 per cent of all households in 1961 to 10 per cent in 1994), but not as sharp as the increase in people living alone. Since the proportion of households with any dependent children at all in them has declined (from 40 per cent of all households in 1961 to 32 per cent in 1994), the effect of the increase in one-parent households is magnified. In 1961, 5 per cent of households with dependent children were headed by a single parent; in 1994 this had risen to 23 per cent, slightly more than one in five of such households.[11] The estimated number of dependent children living in one-parent households increased from about 1 million in 1971 to around 2.3 million in 1992.[12] This is, of course, a "snapshot" picture; one-parent families do not necessarily remain one-parent families any more than two-parent families always remain two-parent families. It has been estimated that the average time spent as a lone parent is just under four years.[13]

There is, moreover, a variety of types of one-parent family and a central feature of our research is the exposure of the differences between them. One group of one-parent families consists of those headed by a *never-married* parent (usually the mother). This has been the *fastest growing* segment of this group since the 1980s, moving from some 90,000 in 1971 to 490,000 in 1992 (an increase of nearly 450 per cent). But the largest *number* of such families are headed by divorced (some 430,000) and separated (about 300,000) mothers (representing an increase of these two groups of about 150 per cent since 1971). Lone fathers head just over 100,000 such families (an increase of 70 per cent since 1971) and widowed mothers about 50,000 (a decrease of 50 per cent since 1971).[14] To these groups must be added one-parent families where the parents formerly lived together but were not married. It is probable that around 10 to 20 per cent of never married single mothers had previously cohabited with the father of their child(ren).[15]

But if we think that a situation where one in five households with children is headed by just one parent represents a serious dislocation of the social structures in which children are brought up, we should remember that in past times families were broken by the death of a parent at perhaps even higher rates. Laslett (1983: 115) cites the records of an English parish in 1688 as showing

---

[11] Utting (1995: 14); *General Household Survey 1994*, Table 2.13.
[12] Utting (1995: 22).
[13] Bradshaw and Millar (1991).
[14] Haskey (1994), (1996c).
[15] Burghes with Brown (1995: 18, 20).

that 35 per cent of all children then alive there had experienced the death of one or other of their parents. Coleman and Salt (1992: 230) remark: "As far as comparable data exist, lone-parent families were just as frequent in the six-teenth and seventeenth centuries as they are now, declining in the nineteenth and early twentieth centuries before increasing to their present level".[16] Nevertheless, it has been suggested that loss of a parent through death pro-duces less socially measurable adverse effects on children than where single parenthood is caused through separation of the parents,[17] so one should be cautious about seeing all forms of single-parenthood in the same way.

The characteristics of lone mothers were examined by Burghes with Brown (1995). They found that those who had never been married were much younger than those who had previously been married (8.6 per cent were under 20 and 37.4 per cent were between 20 and 24 compared to 0.3 per cent and 4.5 per cent for the previously married respectively), which is to be expected in view of the rising age of marriage (discussed below). They were also more likely than the previously married to be living with their own parents (20.9 per cent, compared to 6.1 per cent) and, where they were not living with their parents, they were less likely to be living in owner-occupation (10.5 per cent compared to 43 per cent) and more likely to be in rented premises (80.6 per cent compared to 50.8 per cent). The never-married were also more likely to be receiving Income Support (80 per cent compared to 60 per cent), and where they were in employment, their earnings were lower. In view of this informa-tion, it is perhaps not surprising that never-married lone mothers were less likely to have higher educational qualifications than other lone mothers, and both groups had fewer such qualifications than married couples.

THE FAMILY LIFE-CYCLE

We must now superimpose on the static picture of household structure we have just presented an account of how behaviour has changed, and the ways in which these changes have brought about the present circumstances in which people live.

Changes in marriage patterns

The changes that have occurred in the life-cycle of individuals as far as they relate to that individual's experiences of family living have been vividly illus-trated by Gibson (1994: 117) and we have gratefully adopted his Table 8.1, with the addition of one more generation to bring it even more up-to-date (Table 2.1). This shows that a woman (the "grandmother"), born in 1921, will

---

[16] See also Anderson (1983).
[17] McLanahan and Sandefur (1994: 77); Maclean and Wadsworth (1988).

*Table 2.1: The Changing Life-cycle for Women**

Event and year	Great-great grandmother		Great-grandmother		Grandmother		Mother		Daughter	
	W	H	W	H	W	H	W	H	W	H
	(wife:husband)									
Born	1860	1858	1891	1889	1921	1919	1950	1948	1973	1971
Married										
Year	1886		1916		1945		1972		1998/9	
Age	26	28	25	27	24	26	22	24	25/6	27/8
Husband's death										
Year	1919		1954		1989		2019			
Age	59	61	63	65	68	70	69	71		
Wife's death										
Year	1924		1959		1995		2027			
Age	64	–	68	–	74	–	77	–		
Duration of (in years)										
Marriage	33		38		44		47			
Widowhood	5		5		6		8			

*Adapted from Gibson (1994: Table 8.1).

characteristically have married at age 24, compared to a likely marriage-age of 26 for her great-grandmother (the "great-great-grandmother"), born in 1860. Her daughter (the "mother"), born in 1950, will probably have married at age 22, but *her* daughter, born in 1973, is likely to marry when she is 25 or 26, thus reverting to the nineteenth century pattern, which had prevailed for many centuries. So, in respect of age at marriage, it was the generation born immediately after the Second World War which was unusual and not the present generation.

The immediate post-war generation was also unusual in regard to the *rate* of marriage. From the beginning of the seventeenth century, the proportion of women who did not marry was very high: some 25 per cent. This remained high until a sharp decline at the end of the eighteenth century (down to 4.9 per cent), but the proportion of women who never married rose steadily thereafter to about 14 per cent at the end of the nineteenth century. The casualties of the First World War deprived even more women of the chances of marrying throughout the 1920s, but from the 1930s women began to marry at younger ages and the rate of marriage increased. By the time they were 36 (in 1982), only 5 per cent of women born in 1946 had never married, the lowest proportion ever recorded.[18] Although the 1960s was supposedly the age of libertarian excess, there was a rush to marriage, and at earlier ages, as never

[18] Coleman and Salt (1992: 185).

before. But even during the lifetimes of this generation a remarkable change was occurring.

The decline in marriage and a "demographic transition"

In 1971, following the "decade of marriage" in the 1960s, 10 per cent of girls were already married by the time they were 19; in 1981 this fell to 5.7 per cent, and in 1988 to 3.4 per cent.[19] The Office of Population, Censuses and Surveys has predicted that, while 5 per cent of girls who were aged 16 in 1974 would not have married by the time they reach 50, *a quarter of girls who were 16 in 1990 will never have married by the time they reach that age.*[20] This is in itself a factor of first importance in considering the role of marriage and divorce law. It might be seen as simply a reversion to earlier times and earlier values were it not for the presence of two other factors which are often referred to as constituting a "demographic transition".

The first of these factors is the decline in the death rate. As we can see from Table 2.1, derived from Gibson, the husband of the "great-great-grand-mother" was likely to die at 61, and she at 64. Life expectancy is now 72.1 years for men and 77.8 for women.[21] As Gibson (1994: 127) puts it: "the married man in the age group 35 to 44 had six times greater risk of death in 1900 than his counterpart in 1985". The consequence is that the *potential length of marriages has increased by some 15 years during the course of this century.*

The second factor is the decline in fertility. Fertility had reached its highest level in the very early part of the nineteenth century. A married woman might expect to have six to seven children, though because many women did not marry, the period fertility rate (the average number of children likely to be borne per woman if current age-specific rates persist throughout each woman's lifetime) was just over five.[22] The rate then fell, rose again towards the 1860s, but thereafter began to fall steeply. Despite a short surge after the First World War, the rate, expressed as the average number of children per woman, dropped to a very low point in the early 1930s (1.72), which is insufficient to replace population. These trends occurred throughout Europe, provoking a good deal of concern in an era of nationalist tension. Fertility in Britain improved slightly towards the end of the 1930s, but despite a brief surge after the Second World War, began to drop again, reaching 2.14 in 1951. At this point there occurred the surge known as the "baby boom" which produced 2.4 children per marriage. But after the mid-1960s, the rate fell again, to 1.7 in 1977, and has remained around 1.8 since then, reaching 1.74 for the

---

[19] Coleman and Salt (1992: 179).
[20] OPCS *Monitor* FM2 No. 18. See also Haskey (1995).
[21] Coleman and Salt (1992: 238).
[22] Coleman and Salt (1992: 16–17).

United Kingdom in 1994.[23] 12 per cent of women born in 1944 were childless at age 35. 23 per cent of women born in 1959 were childless at the same age.[24] It should, however, be mentioned that the decline in fertility in the United Kingdom since 1970 has been much more gradual than in most European countries; it has been particularly dramatic in Ireland, Italy and Spain.

One feature of the decline in fertility is that women are having children much later (and if you have children later, you will probably have fewer). The "great-great grandmother" in Table 2.1 would bear some five children (15 per cent of mothers had as many as ten). The "grandmother" in the Table, who married in 1945, would usually have had only two children. If she had married very young, her first child was likely to have been conceived pre-maritally. But this feature began to change after the 1970s. However, despite strong class differentials, both the age at which married mothers have their first child and the distance of this birth from the wedding have increased sharply since 1970. The mean age of the mother at first birth was 23.9 in 1964, and 26.5 in 1994.[25] While a woman is most likely to have a child when she is between 25 and 29, since 1992 a woman is more likely to have a child in her early thirties than in her early twenties.[26] The median interval from the wedding to the birth of the first child was 19 months in 1970 and 27.8 months in 1992.[27] Middle-class women, especially, tend to compress their child-rearing within a narrow range of years.

The combination of these events has significantly altered the experience of family life and it difficult to see how there can be a reversion to the family life-cycle of a couple who married in 1886: late marriage, high fertility and relatively early death. Despite the widespread practice, especially in earlier centuries, for English children to leave their homes during their teens and go either into apprenticeship or domestic service,[28] the "great-great-grand-mother" in Table 2.1 would have lived in a two-generation household for most of her life. She would either have lived with her own parents (or parent), or with another family as a servant or lodger, until she married (in 1886), and her own daughter may well have remained at home until her marriage (in 1916), after which she had only eight more years to live (five of them as a widow). So she might have spent about 90 per cent of her lifetime in a house-hold "family" setting. The young woman marrying today will probably have spent a number of years living alone, or cohabiting without children. If she has children, they would probably pass through her household in about twenty years. She would live in a two-generation household for about half her life.

---

[23] Armitage and Babb (1996: 8).
[24] Armitage and Babb (1996: 9–10).
[25] Armitage and Babb (1996: 9).
[26] *Social Trends 1996* (Central Statistical Office) 60.
[27] Coleman and Salt (1992: 164).
[28] Anderson (1988) estimates that in 1851, 31 per cent of girls and 29 per cent of boys were living away from home.

Alternative forms of partnering: marriage, cohabitation and child-bearing

Low marriage and birth rates do not necessarily imply a reduced incidence of partnering. Many people may still live in a two-person household, but without marrying, and without children. In Britain in 1980, 13 per cent of all women aged 16–19 who were living with a partner were not married to him; in 1989 this had risen to 62 per cent.[29] The equivalent percentages for the age-group 20–24 were 11 per cent and 32 per cent respectively. So a growing slice of partners are not married to one another, especially if they are under 25. In 1979, 11 per cent of all women aged between 18 and 49 were cohabiting with a man to whom they were not married; in 1994 the proportion had risen to 23 per cent.[30]

It seems clear that these "informal unions" have replaced part of the population which in earlier days married one another and we may inquire as to *which* segment or segments of the formerly married population they are replacing. Certainly it is now usual for couples to live together before marrying; only 5 per cent did this in the mid-1960s, whereas 70 per cent did so in the early 1990s. It is even more common for this to happen before a second marriage (90 per cent in the 1990s).[31] It looks as if these cohabitants would in earlier days have married before living together. If we look only at cohabitants with children, the *General Household Survey 1989* revealed that only one in four of cohabitants who had not been previously married had any children (only 7 per cent had two children and 2 per cent had three).[32] So it seems that when cohabitants decide to have a child, especially if more than one, most of them marry. (This does not mean that they necessarily produce a child quickly after they marry). In this respect Britain is different, at least for the present, from a country like Sweden where in 1989 only 72 per cent of women aged 30–34 were married to their partner (compared to 91 per cent in Britain in that year) and where already by the late 1970s it was more usual for a child to be born to an unmarried than to a married couple (although 95 per cent of children were born to a couple who were living together).[33] The difference in the patterns between the countries seems to lie in the attitudes to childbirth. In Britain, childbirth is still the key to converting an unmarried cohabitation into a marriage.

However, for some people, having a child does not lead to marriage. The increase in births outside marriage is well known. In 1964, 7 per cent of children born in England and Wales were born outside marriage. In 1994 it was 32 per cent.[34] "Only" 68 per cent of children are born to a married couple.

---

[29] Kiernan and Estaugh (1993: 61).
[30] *General Household Survey 1994*, Table 2.24.
[31] Haskey (1995: 5, 6).
[32] Kiernan and Estaugh (1993: 11).
[33] Kiernan and Estaugh (1993: 61, 64).
[34] Armitage and Babb (1996: 11, Table 5).

However, of the 216,000 babies born outside marriage in 1994, 55 per cent were registered by both parents at the same address who were therefore probably cohabiting; 20 per cent were registered by both parents at a separate address and nearly 25 per cent were registered by the mother alone.[35] *The large increase in extra-marital births has, in fact, largely been to people who are living together.* In 1984, 8 per cent of children were born to unmarried couples living at the same address; in 1994, 19 per cent of children were born to such couples. Over the same period there was an increase of slightly smaller magnitude of children jointly registered in the names of unmarried parents living at different addresses (from 3 per cent to 6 per cent) and a very small increase of such children registered in the name of the mother only (from 6 per cent to 7 per cent). Put another way, although "only" 68 per cent of children are born within marriage, around 85 per cent are born either to a married couple or to a couple who share the same address.[36] Older parents are more likely to be living at the same address than younger ones.[37]

Yet of the 85 per cent of children born to parents who are apparently living together, the parents of a significant minority (21 per cent[38]) are not married to each other. Certainly, thirty years ago, they would have married. Is this group just like the rest of the married population, except that they have chosen not to formalize their relationship? Both Kiernan and Estaugh (1993) and McRae (1993) have produced interesting evidence that the social circumstances of cohabitants who have children but do not marry are inferior to married people with children. They are less well educated, live in inferior accommodation, have worse employment records and are more likely to have experienced teenage birth. This seems to indicate a class factor; higher social groups tend to marry when they have children. Indeed, there is much less difference in these social indicators between married and unmarried people who do not have children than between those who do have children. As will become apparent, our own data confirm these observations.

However, one must be careful to avoid thinking that unmarried cohabitants form a homogeneous group. Many have been married earlier. In 1979, for example, 20 per cent of divorced women were cohabiting compared to only 7 per cent of never-married women. By 1993 the gap had greatly narrowed, but the proportion of divorcees was still higher (25 per cent as against 23.5 per cent).[39] That is to say, a divorced woman is slightly more likely to enter into a cohabitation outside marriage than a spinster. Many of these divorced women may have children from their former marriage, so their new partnership constitutes a *de facto* stepfamily. These women were once related to their children's father by marriage; though they may have more children by their

---

[35] Armitage and Babb (1996: 11, Table 5).

[36] Armitage and Babb (1996: 11).

[37] Burghes with Brown (1995: 17).

[38] Armitage and Babb (1996: 11, Table 5).

[39] Haskey (1995).

new partner, they are not married to him. It becomes increasingly difficult to assess, in such circumstances, what significance to attribute to the fact that the former union was a marriage.

What happens to these partnerships? They may continue as they are, convert into marriages or break up. There is a very large drop in the proportion of unmarried unions after the woman reaches 25; it falls from 32 per cent to 14 per cent. Whether this will be repeated in future years cannot be known. If it is, then it is likely that many of these partnerships are converting into marriages (or at least, the partners are marrying *someone*, even if not the other partner). The fact that nearly three-quarters of women marrying in the early 1990s had lived with their future husband before marrying him (compared to only 5 per cent in the mid-1960s),[40] suggests that most probably do eventually marry their partner.

Instability in relationships

How frequently do unmarried partnerships break up? It is, unfortunately, not easy to measure this (Murphy (1995)). Haskey (1995) shows that cohabitations between unmarried people have, since 1986, tended to last longer than previously, but this may simply mean that the couple are postponing marrying (or having a child) for longer.[41] There is evidence that unmarried cohabitation in Sweden is less stable than married cohabitation, and McRae's survey of cohabiting *mothers* suggests that couples who have a child while not married, or before marrying, are twice as likely to separate than those who marry before having a child.[42] It would of course not be at all surprising if unmarried cohabitation was far less stable than married cohabitation, especially if it is associated with general social and financial insecurity. As we will see, our data indicates that, at least where unmarried cohabitants have children, their relationships are indeed probably less secure than those of married people.

If the instability of cohabitations by the unmarried is difficult to establish, the instability of marriage is easily indicated by the divorce statistics. A rise in dissolutions (divorce and nullity) in England and Wales from about 600 a year in the years 1901–1910 to 165,018 in 1993 is massive, even taking into account the fact that at the beginning of the century the grounds for divorce were limited and unhappy couples resorted to *de facto* separation instead. Of course, the divorce rate does not mirror precisely the breakdown rate, and fluctuations in divorce often reflect such factors as changes in divorce law and even the availability of legal aid.[43] Nevertheless, Gibson (1994: 133) estimates that the actual *breakdown* rate of marriages may well have increased by a

[40] Haskey (1995: 5).
[41] Haskey (1995: 11).
[42] McRae (1993: 20).
[43] Eekelaar (1984: 12).

factor of five during the course of this century, and statistical projections indicate that at the rates of breakdown apparent in 1993/4 (that is, breakdown rates according to the length of the marriage), 41 per cent of current marriages will ultimately end in divorce.[44]

The apparently inexorable rise in the rate of divorce is somewhat surprising in view of the decline in marriage and the increase in the age of marriage. Marriages have always been more at risk when the couple marry young, so one might expect higher marriage stability when people marry at older ages, and perhaps also if they have lived together before marrying. But this seems not to have occurred, or, at any rate, any effect these factors may have on marriage stability has been delayed.[45] There was, however, a fall in divorces of 4 per cent from 165,018 in 1993 to 153,337 in 1995, and it possible that the divorce rate may now be stabilizing, or even beginning to fall, quite apart from any effect which prospective changes in the law may have.[46] (Such changes may even lead to an immediate *rise* in the rate if couples accelerate divorce proceedings to beat the new system).

Closer examination reveals an even more complex picture than such raw figures suggest. Figure 1 looks at the divorce proneness of four marriage cohorts: people marrying in 1970–74; 1975–79; 1980–84; and 1985–89. It indicates the number of divorces per thousand of all marriages contracted in the four groups of years as they occurred at specific marriage durations. The most revealing comparison is that between the 1970–74 group and the 1975–79 group. Both of these experienced the radical 1971 divorce law reform, though the effectiveness of this reform was enhanced in 1977 when the "special procedure" was extended to all undefended divorces.[47] The 1975–79 cohort shows a consistently higher rate of divorce than the 1970–74 cohort. The rate starts higher and, although both cohorts reach their highest point when the marriages had lasted 4–8 years, the rate of the later cohort is at that point considerably higher than the earlier (by just over four divorces per 1,000 marriages). The peak at 4 years duration is explained by the fact that at that time the members of each group would have emerged from the barrier which then severely restricted access to divorce during the first three years of marriage. But thereafter the rate drops sharply, so that at 6–10 years after the wedding, the rate for each group is almost identical. Thus, the increase in the divorce rate for people marrying in the 1970s is almost entirely an increase experienced during the first 4–8 years of marriage.

---

[44] Haskey (1996: 36).

[45] Haskey (1996: 25, 28).

[46] In fact, the number of divorce *petitions* has fallen from a peak of 191,615 in 1991 to 173,966 in 1995: Lord Chancellor's Department, *Judicial Statistics 1996*, Table 5.5.

[47] The "special procedure", originally introduced in 1973 only for divorces on the ground of two years' separation with consent and where there were no children, allowed a decree to be issued without either of the divorcing parties having to appear in court when the decree was pronounced.

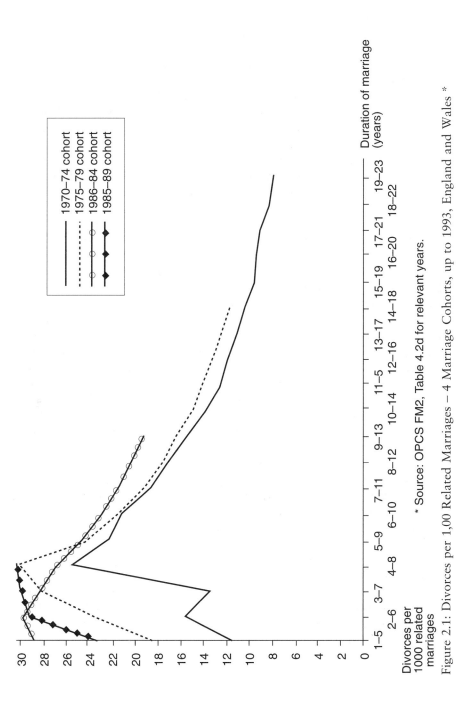

Figure 2.1: Divorces per 1,00 Related Marriages – 4 Marriage Cohorts, up to 1993, England and Wales *

We know less of the fate of people who married in the 1980s because insufficient time has passed to allow comparable data to be collected. But while the 1980–84 cohort experienced a much higher rate of divorce than the earlier ones in the first five years of marriage, this was partly due to the reduction of the three-year bar to a one-year bar in 1984. Thereafter, the rate falls sharply, and although at duration 7–11 years it is higher than the previous two cohorts, the difference (by about three divorces per thousand marriages) is by no means catastrophic. The 1985–89 group starts at a lower rate than the previous group, because there was no "catch-up" effect of the 1984 Act. It may well rise above the previous group at the 3–7 years duration. The overall picture which emerges is that, allowing for the distortions brought about by variations in the restrictions on divorce imposed by the law in the period immediately following the wedding, much the greatest increase in divorce has occurred early in the marriage.[48] Once the 5–9 year duration mark is passed, the difference between the three groups of people marrying between 1970 and 1984 is not very great; perhaps it is even surprisingly low given the social and demographic changes over the past twenty years. One might conclude that, despite the relative ease with which divorce has been obtainable over this period, people do not lightly abandon established relationships.[49]

The length of time between the marriage and divorce has a bearing on the likelihood of the divorce affecting children, and on the likelihood of the couple re-partnering. Slightly more women experience divorce when they are under 35 than over that age, and there has been very little change in this over the past thirty years. But as the age of marriage has risen, more marriages are being dissolved at shorter periods from the wedding, a trend assisted by the reduction in the delay allowed for divorce from three to one year from the wedding.[50] The figures may also have been influenced by the fact that delay between breakdown of the relationship and legal dissolution has also fallen; from some three years in the 1970s to a median period of about six months.[51] This feature will be strongly affected by the new divorce system introduced by the Family Law Act 1996, under which divorce will become impossible before 21 months have elapsed from the wedding (27 months if there are children).

One effect of the increase in divorces within a short marriage duration coupled with lengthening time between marriage and first birth seems to have been that a smaller *proportion* of divorcing couples have dependent children. However, the change has been smaller than one might expect. Slightly over half of divorcing couples in England and Wales have one or more children under 16 (56 per cent in 1994 compared to 62 per cent in 1970). Perhaps the fact that the legal process is now quicker has exaggerated the impression that marriages are actually breaking down quicker than before. In any event, the

[48] See a similar analysis by Haskey (1996).
[49] For further evidence on this, see Smart and Neele (1997).
[50] Haskey (1989).
[51] Coleman and Salt (1992: 200). See also Haskey (1996b).

total number of children involved in divorce has of course increased in line with the overall rise in divorce: from 71,000 in 1970 to 175,961 in 1993.[52]

Complexity of relationships

Divorce is often followed by reconstruction of the family unit in some form. Remarriage has always been important; in 1860, nearly one in five marriages were remarriages. In the middle of this century, the number of remarriages involving at least one divorced partner overtook remarriages involving a widow or widower.[53] The high popularity of marriage in the 1960s affected remarriages as well; they rose by some 40 per cent. However, like first marriages, they have declined since then. But because marriages *as a whole* are now fewer, and divorce is more common, remarriages constitute a high *proportion* of all marriages: in 1993 in some 30 per cent of marriages in England and Wales either the bride or the groom, or both, had been married previously.[54] The fact that a woman has a child from a previous marriage does not decrease her chances of marrying again; in fact, it might slightly enhance them. What matters most is her age.[55] Gibson (1994: 155) suggests that some two-thirds of children who experience divorce will enter into a stepfamily. Since repartnering is likely to produce more children (i.e. stepsiblings), stepfamilies tend to be larger than first families and can even be regarded as a useful mechanism for boosting fertility in an era of population decline.

From our point of view, however, relationship instability is significant for its consequential effects on family structures. It is estimated that in Great Britain in 1991/2, just under 7 per cent of all families with children were stepfamilies. Just under 5 per cent of these were married-couple families and 2 per cent were cohabiting couples. This amounts to just over 1 million children in Great Britain.[56] This is not totally novel, because in past times this frequently occurred through the death of a parent (as the many children's stories featuring stepparents testify) But the context is in fact transformed by the fact that now the absent parent is usually alive and may himself or herself have entered a new family. And the scale, especially in a country with a very high divorce rate, like the USA, is much greater. It has been suggested that by the end of this century, more American children will live in a stepfamily than in a "natural" family.[57] A less dramatic prediction for Great Britain is that 5.5 per cent of children are likely to become stepchildren of a married couple and 6.7 per cent of a cohabiting couple (and some of both) before they reach 16.[58]

---

[52] OPCS, *Marriage and Divorce Statistics*, Series FM2 No. 21, relevant years.
[53] Coleman and Salt (1992: 205).
[54] Haskey (1995: Table 1).
[55] Coleman and Salt (1992: 210).
[56] Haskey (1994b), (1996c: 11).
[57] Wardle (1993).
[58] Haskey (1994b).

Remarriage, or other forms of repartnering, are not only important for children who acquire a stepparent, but also in the effect they may have on the relationship between the stepparent and any children that person might have outside that household. A person who tries to fulfil the parental role to children within the immediate household *and* to a child or children in another household faces serious difficulties. The most obvious problems are financial, for a parent in this position may have some kinds of obligation (legal or social) towards each group of children and it may be difficult to reconcile them. But such a parent also has competing claims on his or her relational commitments. Another important part of this study was to examine how parents dealt with these competing claims.

This dynamic leads back to the earlier discussion of household composition: but it has added the complicating element of the fact that individuals (and especially children) may move from one type of household to another. Complications do not end there because remarriages are even less likely to be successful than first marriages, especially where new children are involved.[59] The risk of breakdown of remarriages appears to be about double that of first marriages.[60] Indeed, as a quarter of divorces feature a party who has been divorced before, there may be a minority of people who enter a sequential *set* of relationships. It seems difficult to discover what size this group is and whether it is increasing. This may not matter very much unless the person concerned is a parent, either a mother taking a child through a succession of stepfathers (and acquiring stepsiblings on the way) or a father, acquiring a variety of child support obligations and relational commitments. As our study will show, for a small group of people, family relationships and resulting obligations can become extremely complicated.

[59] Furstenberg and Spanier (1984).
[60] Gibson (1994: 163).

3

The Basis of Familial Obligations

Why should one person be required to provide support for the welfare of another? As we observed in Chapter 1, moral principles do not provide a complete answer. They need to be mediated through social and institutional mechanisms. What, then, are the legal (or social) mechanisms which result in the acquisition of an obligation on one person to support another?

In examining this question it will help our analysis if we recall the distinction made in Chapter 1 between obligations which impose a *direct* duty on the duty-holder, enforceable by or on behalf of[1] the beneficiary against the duty-holder, and those which are not legally enforceable by the beneficiary but where a third party, by visiting consequences on either the duty-holder or beneficiary, is able *indirectly* to secure or promote their performance. (We call these "direct" and "indirect" obligations). We also use the term "support" widely; primarily it will refer to income payments but the obligation could be met through other forms of resource allocation (for example, lump sum or property transfers).

People may of course enter into associations (for example, religious communities) whose purposes include mutual support. But if we exclude such arrangements, and we also set aside obligations which have a specific contractual basis, there seem to be three main contexts which give rise to support obligations: marriage, blood relationship (including parenthood) and sharing a common household. The social information provided in the last chapter has indicated how this century has seen significant changes in respect to all three of these features of our society. We need, therefore, to look closely at the way in which these categories interact in generating obligations.

MARRIAGE

Direct support obligations

Marriage has traditionally been seen to be the legal mechanism which has directly created legal obligations, not only between the adult parties, but also between them and their children. However the extent to which marriage *in itself* was and is either necessary or sufficient to create a direct support

---

[1] The child support obligation is usually enforced on behalf of the child by the person looking after it.

obligation between family members is very problematic. For while the spouses are living together, it seems that the legal obligation of support runs parallel with an underlying social obligation which is assumed to exist when a couple living in a domestic relationship share a household.

As we have described elsewhere,[2] although the rights which a husband acquired with respect to his wife on marrying were held to carry with them obligations to provide her with sustenance (that is, the law recognized a direct support obligation) the common law gave no effective remedies to wives to enforce the obligation while they were living together. But if the wife had been cast out, she might have been able to bind him indirectly by allowing a creditor who had provided her with "necessary" purchases (assuming she was able to obtain them on credit) to recover the costs from the husband, at least if she had no alternative means for supporting herself. Before 1858 the Ecclesiastical Courts could make alimony orders when granting separation decrees (known as divorce *a mensa et thoro*), but before 1813[3] these were unenforceable. In any case they required proof of specific offences (adultery, cruelty or unnatural acts) against the husband. Later, an innocent wife who was either subjected to assault[4] or who had been deserted[5] (provided she remained "chaste") could apply for a maintenance order from a magistrates' court, which (until 1968[6]) was subject to a (low) upper limit. The Magistrates' Courts (now called "Family Proceedings Courts") may still make maintenance orders in favour of a spouse if the other has "failed to provide reasonable maintenance" for him or her, but any order lapses if the couple have been living together for more than six months.[7] The jurisdiction was mainly used to obtain support from absent fathers,[8] and its use declined sharply since divorce became more readily available after 1971. Furthermore, in this respect the courts' role has now been taken over by the Child Support Agency (see pp. 38–9 below).[9]

For practical purposes, then, the support obligation between married people who are living together is enforced *indirectly*, in the manner described below (p. 32) rather than directly. However, where married people have separated, the advent of judicial divorce allowed the fact that the parties *had been married* to become a new basis for directly imposing support obligations. The

[2] Eekelaar and Maclean (1986: Ch 1).

[3] Ecclesiastical Courts Act 1813.

[4] Matrimonial Causes Act 1878.

[5] Married Women (Maintenance in the Case of Desertion) Act 1886.

[6] Maintenance Orders Act 1968.

[7] Domestic Proceedings and Magistrates Courts Act 1978, ss. 1, 25.

[8] It was found that, as long ago as 1966, 82 per cent of a sample of women applying for maintenance orders in magistrates' courts had children: McGregor, Blom-Cooper and Gibson (1970: 76).

[9] Maintenance orders between spouses which are made under the Matrimonial Causes Act 1973, s. 27, may be enforced while the couple are living together. But orders under this section are very rare; only 51 applications were made in 1989: P.M. Bromley and N.V. Lowe (eds.) *Bromley's Family Law* (1992) 694. We do not know whether the parties were living together in those cases.

Matrimonial Causes Act 1857 allowed the divorce courts to make orders against the former husband for the support of the former wife. However, the courts were given a discretion to exercise their powers as they deemed to be reasonable in the circumstances[10] and the cases show that the mere fact of having been married was not a sufficient ground for an order for financial provision. If a wife was guilty, she might receive modest support, but only if this was necessary to prevent her becoming destitute and she had no alternative means of support. If she was innocent, however, the courts, after some hesitation, were prepared to make maintenance orders according to their assessment of the merits of the case, and one reason for doing so was to provide partial recompense to wives for loss of their property which had passed to their husbands on the marriage.

This did not, therefore, mean that an "innocent" wife was guaranteed support at the level she received during the marriage. However, in 1969 the Law Commission, on the basis of very insecure legal foundations,[11] recommended that the courts should endeavour to "place the parties in the financial position in which they would have been if the marriage had not broken down and each had properly discharged his or her financial obligations and responsibilities towards the other" (sometimes called the "minimal loss principle") and this recommendation became law in 1971.[12] This attempt to project the obligations of marriage beyond its dissolution was a major error, especially as it accompanied the commencement of the reformed divorce law of 1971. This law accepted the principle that divorce should be available if the relationship had broken down irretrievably. Allegations of fault were retained only as among varieties of evidence on which such breakdown could be held to be established. It seemed quite illogical to say that the marriage itself could be dissolved if the relationship was over while retaining obligations which arose from the marital state alone.[13]

In fact, the courts rarely applied the minimal loss principle, and it was formally removed by the Matrimonial and Family Proceedings Act 1984. Our previous research had shown that, as a matter of post-divorce economics, the position of childless couples after their divorce was very different from that faced by divorcing couples who had children. For the former, there was little difference between the economic profile after divorce of the men and women. But for the latter, only 18 per cent of those women who still had dependent children living with them after divorce had household income above the official "poverty" line, compared to 46 per cent of the men who had had dependent children at the time of the divorce.[14] These economic facts are

---

[10] Matrimonial Causes Act 1857, s. 32.

[11] See Eekelaar and Maclean (1986: Ch 3).

[12] Matrimonial Proceedings and Property Act 1970, s. 5(1); subsequently Matrimonial Causes Act 1973, s. 25.

[13] See Gray (1977: 321).

[14] Similar disparities have been shown in other countries. For a summary of the research findings, see Eekelaar and Maclean (1994: 6–7).

reflected in the legal dynamics. An order for continuing support after divorce was found in only 11 per cent cases where there were no dependent children, and a voluntary arrangement in only 2 per cent. By contrast, continuing support orders had been made in 55 per cent and voluntary arrangements in a further 10 per cent of the divorces involving dependent children.[15] Not surprisingly, fewer of the childless had consulted a lawyer (61 per cent) than those who had had children (87 per cent); only 9 per cent of the former had received legal aid, compared to 63 per cent of those with children.

A review of the case law in 1979[16] showed that the principles actually adopted by the courts (that is, the law *as (generally) interpreted*) (see p. 5 above) were consistent with this reality. There were found to be two major principles, ranked in the following order: first, that adequate provision must be made to ensure the support and accommodation of the children of the marriage and, second, that "provision must be made to meet the needs of each spouse which have been occasioned by the marriage breakdown. Thus, a spouse who has adequate capital or income, or is capable of earning it, will not be favoured but a spouse may demonstrate needs mainly (i) by taking on the care of the child or children; (ii) by having to adapt to the labour market after a lengthy stay at home: thus requiring "transitional" or "rehabilitative" help and (iii) by being too old, at marriage breakdown, to become fully self-supporting". In addition to this, distribution according to "some kind of proprietal entitlement" sometimes occurred by taking into account "contributions", but this played a "secondary" and "uncertain" role in relation to the needs principle.

As far as legal doctrine is concerned, the Matrimonial and Family Proceedings Act 1984 left the resolution of post-divorce financial and property conflicts largely to the discretion of the courts, although various provisions encourage courts to promote the financial independence of the parties and finality of the settlement. In fact, a further review in 1996 found that the approach of the courts after 1984 differed little from their approach in the 1970s,[17] although the desire to maintain adequate housing for children was more marked, and there was a greater inclination to expect women who were no longer looking after children to seek employment. In summary, it appears that modern justifications for imposing post-divorce support obligations fall into two categories. The first addresses the disparities between the parties' resources after divorce. The one reason above all others for redressing this disparity is the fact that the parties are the parents to a common child or children and have at some point jointly engaged in their upbringing. Here the

---

[15] Eekelaar and Maclean (1986: 90–1). Similar findings have been made in other research, referred to *loc cit* at 92.

[16] Eekelaar (1979).

[17] Eekelaar (1996). This report was based on interviews with registrars (now District Judges), reported in Eekelaar (1991), analysis of reported cases and interviews with a small number of solicitors.

parental relationship seems more significant than marriage as a basis for justifying a support obligation. Another reason is that the mere fact of having lived together provides a reason for redress which gains in strength according to the length of the cohabitation. While it is true that the law allows redress only where the parties have in fact been married, the courts are prepared to consider the whole period of time when they lived together as a single unit, even if they were married for only part of it.[18] Here *having shared a household* appears to have a larger effect than merely being married in the generation of the obligation. The obligation which is generated, however, is primarily one to provide for the "reasonable needs" of the less well-off former partner, assessed on a highly discretionary basis.[19]

The second category grounds redress on the basis that one party holds assets to which the other has contributed. However, this category operates uncertainly in English law. While contributions of a domestic nature may establish a claim to redress, they will normally be seen as establishing a claim to domestic but not, for example, to business assets (unless there had been direct participation in running the business).[20] It is also unclear how far such contributions establish an entitlement of a proprietary nature, or whether they can ignored if the contributor's "needs" are met in other ways.[21]

The conclusion must be that, as far as obligations during the parties' lifetime is concerned,[22] while the fact of having been married is a necessary condition in order to allow the courts to exercise jurisdiction to confer certain rights and duties on a couple when they separate, that fact is not in itself a complete and sufficient reason for bringing such obligations into existence. Being parents may be a more important feature than being married, and having shared a household might also contribute to the basis of the obligation. However, as will be seen, neither the facts of having shared a household nor of being parents (even if coupled with sharing a home) will in themselves give as full protection as is available to people who have shared a household, are parents *and* are (or have been) married.

---

[18] *B.* v. *B. (Consent Order: Variation)* [1995] 1 FLR 9; *W.* v. *W.* [1995] 2 FLR 259.

[19] See *Dart* v. *Dart* [1996] 2 FLR 286, where the Court of Appeal upheld the trial judge's decision to award a "good" wife and mother of a fourteen-year marriage £9 million out of the husband's resources of £400 million, although Peter Gibson LJ said that he thought it to be "on the low side".

[20] See *W.* v. *W.* [1996] 3 FCR 641; Contrast however the approach of Purchas LJ in *Vicary* v. *Vicary* [1992] 2 FLR 271.

[21] Contrast *Smith* v. *Smith* [1991] 2 All ER 306 with *Schuller* v. *Schuller* [1990] 2 FLR 193.

[22] This analysis applies only to relationship while the parties are alive. A survivor who was married to someone dying intestate is in a better position than one who was not so married, but this may be explained as an attempt to reflect what the deceased parties were likely to have wished.

Indirect obligations

Although the common law was reticent in directly enforcing a husband's duty to support his wife, the duty was given legal effect indirectly in a statute of 1740 which allowed justices to seize the goods and enter the land of a man who left his wife and children and to provide for them out of the sale and rents,[23] and in 1834 it was provided that any poor relief given to her should be treated as a loan recoverable from him.[24] The Finer Report (1974) described the system of indirect enforcement of family obligations through the poor law as the "Third System of Family Law". However, the system did not extend to divorced spouses (though in the early days of divorce very few poor people were likely to experience divorce) and this is still the case. *Being married* is therefore a basis for indirectly enforcing a support obligation where a separated but still married person receives social security benefits and the Department of Social Security reclaims those benefits from the other spouse.[25] However for most practical purposes benefits are recovered only where they are paid to a separated mother who is bringing up children. In that case the Child Support Agency will normally raise an assessment against the absent father. Such claims are made simply on the basis of parenthood; it matters not whether the parents are still married, or divorced, or never had been married or even whether they have ever shared a common household.

There are other ways in which the obligation is indirectly recognized. Income Support is payable to unemployed people without adequate means, but an unemployed wife cannot claim on her own behalf even if her (working) husband is giving nothing to her because claims are made on behalf of a family unit. However this is only true while the couple are members of the same household.[26] This denial can be seen both as recognition of the fact that married people living together usually share their resources and as a means of putting pressure on spouses who are living together to fulfil their legal obligation (as spouses) to support one another and their assumed social obligation (as home-sharers) to do the same. However, if the couple separate, other than temporarily, then each can claim Income Support in their own right[27] even though the legal obligation of one to support the other continues (at least if not abrogated by the "misbehaviour" of the potential beneficiary). This indicates that, in this situation, the state has chosen not to attempt to enforce the legal obligation indirectly. So perhaps even where the spouses are living together the state is really indirectly enforcing the assumed *social* duty of support between home-sharers rather than the legal duty between spouses. This

---

[23] 13 Geo. 2, c. 24 (1740); later, Vagrancy Act 1824, s. 3.
[24] Poor Relief Act 1834, s. 56.
[25] Social Security Administration Act 1992, s. 106.
[26] Social Security Contributions and Benefits Act 1992, ss. 134(2) and 137 (1).
[27] See Ogus, Barendt and Wikeley (1995: 471).

interpretation is supported by the rules applicable to unmarried cohabitants (p. 46 below).

(p. 46 below)

THE PARENT-CHILD RELATIONSHIP

Marriage and parental status

Just as marriage is not a sufficient basis for establishing a support obligation between adults, so it appears that it is not a necessary element in creating a legal relationship between parents and children. This was not always the case. While the early law books devoted many pages to the law of marriage, the space given to the law governing the relationships between parents and children was sparse. Where such relationships were dealt with, it was strongly linked to the parents' marital relationship. Blackstone (1765), for example, begins his discussion of this area of law by distinguishing between "two sorts" of children: "legitimate, and spurious, or bastards".[28] A parent's duties to legitimate children are "their maintenance; their protection; and their education". Although the duty of maintenance is said to be a "principle of natural law" laid on parents "in bringing them into the world", Blackstone later firmly links this to the legal institution of marriage, "the main end and design of marriage ... being to ascertain and fix upon some certain person, to whom the care, the protection, the maintenance and the education of the children should belong".[29]

Blackstone's ensuing discussion in fact reveals how imperfectly the law enforced the duties of care, protection and maintenance. In fact, the relationship was primarily one which underwrote the authority of the father. Nevertheless, under this ordering it was within the context of marriage that the standard features of the legal parent-child relationship were to be found. According to English law, authority over a legitimate child vested in the father only. The mother obtained equal rights only in 1973.[30] But even in Blackstone's day, children born outside marriage were not entirely deprived of legal relationships, though these were very imperfect. He wrote that "although bastards are not looked upon as children to any civil purposes, yet the ties of nature, of which maintenance is one, are not so easily dissolved". He pointed to statutory provisions allowing justices of the peace to make orders against mothers or fathers of children being supported by the parish, or even for their goods to be seized if they "ran away from the parish", thereby indicating that it was not so much the ties of nature, but the protection of parish funds, which provided the basis for these obligations. He says

---

[28] Blackstone (1775: 446).
[29] Blackstone (1775: 455).
[30] Guardianship Act 1973.

nothing of any duty to "protect" or to "educate" children born outside marriage.

Indeed, children born outside marriage had no legally recognized guardians. Neither their mother nor their father had this status[31] and neither had a "right" to the custody of the child.[32] In 1841 Maule J. asked rhetorically: "how does the mother of an illegitimate child differ from a stranger?",[33] a statement which Lord Herschell later considered put "bluntly the legal doctrine".[34] The Court of Chancery, however, claimed to offer such children the same care and attention as children born within marriage, and would appoint guardians for them, but stopped short of including them within the expression "natural children" when construing wills and settlements, and would not recognize any "natural" duty of parents to maintain an illegitimate child, even indirectly.[35]

This brief sketch of our earlier law shows the linkage between a strong marriage law and dividing children between those of legitimate and those of illegitimate status. In his comparative survey of parent-child relationships, Harry D. Krause (1976) cited Brinton's comment that "bastardy and marriage in this world are quite complementary—you cannot have the one without the other" and added that "perplexingly, illegitimacy seems to defy solution so long as there is marriage". So long as the "main end" of marriage is, as Blackstone claimed, to define parent-child relationships, the legal relationship between children born outside marriage and their parents will indeed be imperfect, and to the extent that the legal relationship between such children and their parents grows closer to that between married parents and their children, so the "main end" of marriage, as seen by Blackstone, begins to fade.

By the late nineteenth century, the common law's refusal to recognize rights between a non-marital child and its mother was becoming obsolete. In 1891 Lord Herschell argued that the fact that the Poor Law imposed duties on the mother of an illegitimate child "appears to me to involve a right to its custody".[36] This was not a strong argument because similar duties were not seen to confer rights on the father, but by that time the Courts of Equity had evolved a preference for giving custody of such children to their mother, partly because they applied the principle that they should do what was in the best interests of the children. Thus the position remained until the Family Law Reform Act 1969 granted reciprocal succession rights between illegitimate children and their parents (but not other relatives) and reversed the rule of construction confining the words "child" or "children" in wills and settlements to legitimate children. The Children Act 1975 however confirmed the

---

[31] See Chambers (1842: 73).
[32] Simpson (1875: 127, citing *In re White*, 10 LT 349).
[33] *Re Lloyd* (1841) 3 M. & G. 547.
[34] *Barnardo v. McHugh* [1891] AC 388 at 398.
[35] Chambers (1842: 14, 115).
[36] *Barnardo v. McHugh* [1891] AC 388 at 398.

position that had been reached at the end of the nineteenth century whereby parental "rights" over an illegitimate child were confined to the mother.[37]

In 1979 the Law Commission published a Working Paper[38] which pointed to the growing illegitimacy rate since the Second World War. Between the end of the war and 1960, about 5 per cent of births each year were recorded as being illegitimate; in 1977 it had reached 9.1 per cent. The Commission noted the legal "discrimination" against illegitimate children. This was mainly found in very inferior provisions for enabling the mother to obtain support for the child from the father, but extended to continued restrictions on succession (when compared to legitimate children), the inability to obtain United Kingdom citizenship if born outside the United Kingdom even if both parents were United Kingdom citizens, and the non-recognition of any legal relationship between the child and its father. The Final Report of 1982[39] proposed reforms which were substantially enacted in the Family Law Reform Act 1987. This enunciated the significant new principle that:

> "in this Act and enactments and instruments made after the coming into force of this section, references (however expressed) to any relationship between two persons shall, unless the contrary intention appears, be construed without regard to whether or not the father and mother of either of them, or the father and mother of any person through whom the relationship is deduced, have or had been married to each other at any time".[40]

So for most purposes, including succession,[41] marriage does not affect the legal relationship between children and parents.

A new concept: "parental responsibility"

The Family Law Reform Act 1987 retained the distinction between marital and non-marital children as regards acquisition of British citizenship if born outside the United Kingdom and, more importantly, also kept the distinction between the legal relationship a mother has with her child born outside marriage (which is no different from the one she has with her marital child) and that of the father to his non-marital child. This policy was retained in the Children Act 1989 which created the concept of "parental responsibility" and enacted that, while married parents each have parental responsibility regarding their children, only the mother of a non-marital child automatically has parental responsibility. The child's father can acquire it only by agreement with the mother or by court order.[42]

---

[37] Children Act 1975, s. 85(7).

[38] Law Commission (1979).

[39] Law Commission (1982).

[40] Family Law Reform Act 1987, s. 1(1).

[41] Family Law Reform Act 1987, s. 18. But if the parents were not married, the father is presumed not to have survived a deceased child unless proved to the contrary: s. 18(2).

[42] Children Act 1989, s. 2. See further p. 146 below.

How far does it really matter if an unmarried father does not have parental responsibility? On the face of it, the absence of parental responsibility places him in a precarious position in some important respects. For example, he cannot remove the child from a local authority which is looking after the child on a voluntary basis, unless the authority agrees,[43] nor is his consent necessary for the child's adoption (though his views must be sought if he is supporting the child and he can always be made a party to the proceedings) or the child's marriage (if the child marries under 18). If he separates from the child, leaving the child with the mother, she can take the child abroad, or even change its name, without his consent, which she could not do if he had parental responsibility.[44] On the other hand, should a local authority hold the child on an Emergency Protection Order, or under some other provision, it must consult the child's parents (whether married to each other or not) and not only allow contact between the child and the parents unless ordered to the contrary but also try to "promote" such contact.[45] If an unmarried father disagrees with the mother (or anyone else) over matters concerning the child's upbringing, and this cannot be resolved in any other way, he is entitled to apply for any of the orders a court may make concerning the upbringing of the child[46] without first having to obtain the leave of the court.

Yet these are rather exceptional circumstances, and in the case of going abroad and changing the child's name, the father can always challenge the decision by applying for a court order. Whether having parental responsibility makes any difference as regards day-to-day matters is more difficult to assess because the concept itself is elusive. The Children Act 1989 defines it as:

> "all the rights, duties, powers, responsibilities and authority which by law a parent of a child has in relation to the child and his property".[47]

Essentially, this means doing those things which it is necessary for a parent who has day-to-day care of the child to do in bringing up the child (what we may call "parenting").[48] Parental responsibility is a useful concept because it may sometimes be acquired by someone who is not the child's parent (for example, a foster-parent, or a grandparent) but who is actually bringing up the child. With parental responsibility, such a person can then sign necessary consent forms for school trips, and even take more significant decisions regarding the child, with the same authority as a parent who has such respon-

---

[43] Although if he brings court proceedings to have the child handed over to him, and he poses no threat to the child, his position as the child's father will put him in a strong position over any "strangers in blood" who may be looking after the child: *Re O.* [1992] 1 FLR 77.

[44] Children Act 1989, s. 13.

[45] Children Act 1989, ss. 22(4), 34(1), 44(13), Sch. 2, para. 15(1).

[46] These are "residence" orders (stating with whom the child may live), "contact" orders, "prohibited steps orders" (orders regulating the way someone with parental responsibility exercises that responsibility) and "special issue orders" (decisions on particular issues): Children Act 1989, s. 8.

[47] Children Act 1989, s. 3(1).

[48] See the lists in Bainham (1993: 96–7) and Barton and Douglas (1995: 114).

sibility. But the fact that a *parent* who does not have parental responsibility does not have *all* the rights of parenthood does not mean that he has none, as we have seen. In particular, an unmarried father has a greater claim to bring up his child than a non-parent (provided this would not be injurious to the child), whether he has parental responsibility or not.[49] It would be very odd, therefore, if such a father who was bringing up his extra-marital child alone somehow lacked authority to make decisions (for example, regarding medical treatment and educational choices).

What, then, does parental responsibility give to such a man? He would be in a safer position regarding those few exceptional events mentioned above (adoption, withdrawing his child from voluntary accommodation from a local authority against the authority's wishes). Beyond that, although parental responsibility has been said to confer a "status", this seems to go little further than amounting to a "stamp of approval" on the exercise of his parental role.[50] It would not give him any better right to make these day-to-day decisions than the mother, because the Children Act 1989 provides that any person with parental responsibility may act alone in meeting that responsibility without any other such person.[51] It does not give him a right to be consulted over such matters. The upshot seems to be that while it can hardly be unlawful for an unmarried father who does not have parental responsibility to take those actions associated with "parenting" the child when he is in a practical position to take them, this is a *de facto* rather than *de iure* authority. So while a doctor could safely act on his authorization of medical treatment for the child, he might equally legitimately refuse to do so. The father's actions lack the blessing of the law because the law is not prepared to make the assumption, as it does in the case of married parents, that it is appropriate for an unmarried father to act as the child's parent. He needs first either to obtain the mother's agreement, or prove his commitment to the child before a court.[52] The implications of this distinction are, however, minimal in practice, and insofar as an unmarried father is actually bringing up a child, the distinction makes little sense. We will return to this point when we have fully considered our data (p. 146 below).

The parental support obligation

Direct obligations
With respect to child support, the common law imposed no direct obligation on the father, whether he was married to the mother or not.[53] We will

[49] *Re O.* [1992] 1 FLR 77.
[50] *Re S. (Parental Responsibility)* [1995] 2 FLR 648.
[51] Children Act 1989, s. 2(7). Eekelaar, in (1996) 112 *Law Quarterly Review* 233.
[52] *Re H (a minor) (Parental Responsibility)* [1993] 1 FLR 484.
[53] Blackstone (1775: 446–7); Eekelaar and Maclean (1986: Ch 2); Eekelaar and Maclean (1988); Barton and Douglas (1995: 147).

consider the indirect duties created by public law below (pp. 41–4). However, ironically, a father first acquired a direct support duty towards his child in 1844 when the Poor Law Amendment Act 1844 permitted an unmarried mother to obtain a magistrates' court order against the father requiring him to support both herself and her illegitimate child.[54] Later statutes extended this entitlement to married women[55] and the divorce courts had always been able to make provision for the maintenance of children by formerly married parents. But the procedures and remedies available to unmarried women were subject to a variety of restrictions (for example, confinement to magistrates' courts, unavailability of secured or lump sum orders) which did not apply to married women until the Family Law Reform Act 1987 assimilated them with those available for marital children. These were re-enacted in the Children Act 1989.[56]

However, the law governing the duty to make *income* payments to children was transformed by the Child Support Act 1991, which, apart from exceptional cases,[57] codifies the legal support obligations of all parents towards their children, irrespective of parental status, and transfers the assessment and enforcement of the obligations from the courts to the Child Support Agency. However, these obligations only arise when a parent leaves the household. The legal obligations which exist while the household is intact are (for the most part) indirect in nature, and are discussed later (pp. 41–4).

The Child Support Act 1991 clearly articulates a legal obligation of support: "each parent of a qualifying child is responsible for supporting him."[58] A "qualifying child" is a dependent child who is living apart from one or both of his parents. [59] The person with the care of the child may apply for a maintenance assessment regarding a qualifying child. The extent of the obligation is fixed by a formula. Under this formula a target liability (the "maintenance requirement") is created which is equivalent to the social security payments to which the debtor's child and its carer are entitled (whether they are receiving them or not). The award is set at half the debtor's assessable income (i.e., net income less certain "exempts"); if that amount is lower than the target, he pays that amount. But if the amount exceeds the target, the debtor pays the

---

[54] See Finer and O.R. McGregor (1974).

[55] See the full discussion in Eekelaar and Maclean (1986: Ch 2).

[56] Children Act 1989, s. 15 and Sch. 1.

[57] Disabled children, school-fees and "top up" orders for richer parents.

[58] Child Support Act 1991, s. 1(1).

[59] The Child Support Act 1995 restates this obligation in a more general form (although it arises only in the context of the child support scheme; i.e. when one parent is living separately from the child). Under that Act a child support officer can, in limited circumstances, permit a "departure" from the amount of child support determined by the child support formula. In deciding whether to allow this, the officer must have regard to the principles that "parents should be responsible for maintaining their children whenever they can afford to do so" and that "where a parent has more than one child, his obligation to maintain any one of them should be no less of an obligation than his obligation to maintain any other of them": Child Support Act 1995, s. 5, inserting s. 28E into the Child Support Act 1991.

target sum and an additional amount based on lower percentages of the remaining assessable income. In 1995 a general "cap" was imposed confining the maximum amount to 30 per cent of the debtor's net income.

Provision is also made for taking into account the income of the person looking after the child if it exceeds a certain amount. If that person is earning considerably more than the absent parent, the absent parent's liability will be small.

It is difficult far a formula-based system to allocate the direct support obligation between a child's parents fairly. It would need to take into account a wide range of circumstances, such as the extent to which the absent parent had already made provision in the form of capital and property settlement or makes provision in other forms, perhaps including expenses incurred in keeping contact with the child; and whether the carer had acquired other means of support (for example, from a new partner); and whether the absent parent's legal obligation conflicted with new familial obligations (social or legal) he may have acquired. The reason is that a child is a member of a *household*, with its internal network of legal and social support obligations, and part of the considerations of fairness involves a comparison between the households of each parent and their respective *social* as well as legal obligations (i.e. issues of corrective justice[60]). But these considerations were excluded in the original form of the scheme, partly because it was thought that their inclusion would create too much complexity or introduce an element of discretion, and partly because the scheme was largely seen by its creators as creating an obligation on the absent parent towards the state to reimburse the social security fund for its support of the children. Thus the scheme is a significant means for indirectly enforcing the support obligation, and is discussed further in the context of indirect obligations (see p. 41 below).

But the courts may be used for enforcing direct child support obligations in cases falling outside the jurisdiction of the Agency. These include not only the special cases of children with disabilities and the payment of school fees, but also cases where the operation of the various limits on the orders available under the scheme leave sufficient funds with the absent parent to permit a "top-up" order through the courts. Also, the courts retain jurisdiction to make child support orders when these are in identical terms to a written agreement between the parties.[61] This power, originally intended to be temporary, allows the parents, where they can agree, to make adjustments which reflect the circumstances of their households and to incorporate the result of the agreement into a consent order made by a court. However, should the parent who is looking after the child seek to receive social security benefits, the agreement is vulnerable to be overridden by an assessment by the Agency.[62]

---

[60] For fuller accounts, see Maclean and Warman (1997); Eekelaar (1997).
[61] Child Support Act 1991, s. 8(5).
[62] *Crozier* v. *Crozier* [1994] Fam 114.

In the rare event of someone wishing directly to enforce the support oblig-ation while the defaulting parent is still living in the family, it will be neces-sary to make use of the Children Act 1989, which, like the Child Support Act 1991, also applies irrespective of the parents' marital relationship.[63] The Children Act is also important because the Child Support Act deals only with income payments. Prior to 1987, property transfers could only be ordered between married parents when they obtained a decree of divorce or judicial separation. But the Family Law Reform Act 1987 (now re-enacted in the Children Act 1989) allowed courts to order a "settlement to be made for the benefit of a child" of property to which either parent was entitled, or that such property be transferred to the other parent "for the benefit of the child" or to the child itself, regardless of the parents' marital status.[64] In recommending that the courts be given these powers, the Law Commission expressly sought to equate the position of separated unmarried parents with separated parents who were formerly married:

> "It seems to us . . . that if unmarried parents separate it is only right that the court should be able to make any appropriate order in favour of a child of theirs, just as it could make an order if the child's parents were in the process of divorce or judi-cial separation. The parents' relationship may well have lasted as long as many mar-riages which end in divorce, and the child's financial position may equally need to be secured".[65]

Although the Commission went on to express the expectation that these powers would not be frequently exercised, the reform has further diminished the legal significance that parents who separate have been married. For exam-ple, the courts have interpreted the word "benefit" widely. It does not mean that the children must receive a *financial* benefit. So one parent's interest in a house can be ordered to be transferred to the other if the result would be that the other could then live there with the children because this would "benefit" the children,[66] just as courts often do when the parents have been married.

There is, however, a limitation to this power. The courts will not order a parent to transfer property in such a way as to benefit his or her children once they have passed the age of 18 or have finished full-time education. So if the home is owned by the father and the court wants to keep the children in the house with their mother, it can order the house to be transferred to the mother to hold as trustee while the children are under 18 or undergoing full-time edu-cation (she living there rent-free during that period), but it must go back to the father after that.[67] This puts an unmarried parent in a weaker position against the other parent than a married (or formerly married) parent. Hence,

---

[63] Domestic Proceedings and Magistrates Courts Act 1978, s. 25; Matrimonial Causes Act 1973, s. 27(1); Children Act 1989, Sch. 1. Barton and Douglas (1995: 147).

[64] Family Law Reform Act 1987, ss. 12–14; Children Act 1989, Sch. 1, para. 1(2)(d).

[65] Law Commission (1982) para. 6.6.

[66] *K. v. K.* [1992] 1 WLR 530; *Pearson v. Franklin* [1994] 1 WLR 370.

[67] *A. v. A.* [1994] 1 FLR 657.

in *T* v. *S*.[68] a District Judge had ordered that, when the children were no longer dependent, the house should be sold and the proceeds distributed to the five children, it being understood that they would use it to buy a house for their mother. The order was overturned on appeal and the proceeds had to revert to the father, a man of considerable wealth, because of the rule that children could not benefit from the order once they were independent. But the judge remarked:

> "The sadness here is that, after a long and seemingly happy relationship, this mother of five children, never having been married to their father, has no rights against him of her own. She has no right to be supported by him in the short, still less the long, term; no right in herself to have even a roof over her head".

As the law currently stands, therefore, neither being a parent nor having shared a household for many years sets up direct obligations *between the parents* (see p.45). Marriage remains a pre-condition for such obligations. However, being married makes little or no difference with respect to the support obligation directly owed by parents to their children, whether this is expressed in terms of income payments or a property settlement.

Indirect obligations

Prior to the sixteenth century, people who lacked household support and who were in need might find help in religious establishments, or through the good-will of the manor houses. The Poor Law Act of 1601 consolidated developments in the late sixteenth century which passed this function over to the community through the parish. While the community widely accepted responsibility for those who fell outside the household economy,[69] it also sought to strengthen social familial support obligations by giving them legal force and enforcing them indirectly. Parents were required to support their children and grandparents their grandchildren. But children were required to support their parents only if the parents were "poor, old, blind, lame and impotent" and could not work. This may be because, unlike other European countries, it seems that there was no social rule in England obligating children who had left home to provide any income to their parents.[70] In Scotland, obligations extended to the wider kin recognized by Scots common law (including siblings and in-laws).

It was stated earlier that the Child Support Act 1991 is now the primary expression of the legal obligation placed directly upon parents to support their children, although it applies only where a parent has left the child. The Act is also the primary vehicle by which the state *indirectly* enforces the support

---

[68] [1994] 2 FLR 883.

[69] Coleman and Salt (1992), citing Newman Brown, mention a parish in Hertfordshire where between 1641 and 1701, 27% of the population was at any one time receiving welfare paid for by about 43% of the population. See Thomson (1986).

[70] See Macfarlane (1986: 79–85).

obligation. A parent with care who receives certain social security benefits[71] may be required to authorize a child support officer to make an application against the absent parent. She risks losing some of the benefit if she refuses to co-operate. Insofar as the scheme has been used for this purpose, it operates as a measure for re-distributing costs between the community and the absent parent (distributive justice) rather than between the parents themselves, and for this reason, in its original form, it did not take into account a variety of matters (see p. 39 above) which were properly relevant to its functioning as a means of promoting corrective justice between the parents. Reforms were therefore introduced in 1995 which allow the formula-based assessment to be modified to take into account those matters.[72]

The Act is therefore an important example of an attempt to make more rigorous a *legally* defined familial obligation (income support of a child by its biological parents) by indirect means. But the state can also use indirect means to attempt to bolster what it deems to be appropriate *social* obligations. For example, there is evidence that, at least before the nineteenth century, poor law relief would be provided for a poor, elderly, person even if he or she was living in a child's household.[73] But during the nineteenth century poor law authorities developed a "household means test" under which the income of *all* relatives living in a household was expected to contribute towards the support of a pauper who was living with them, whether or not they fell within the legal definition of those liable to support the pauper. This allowed a greater burden of support to fall on families and reduced the costs of enforcement. As M.A. Crowther (1982) has explained:

> "(g)uardians assumed that families would make up the difference between outdoor relief and a subsistence income rather than see a relative starve or enter the workhouse".[74]

This tactic was formalized in the 1920s and 1930s in relation to support for the unemployed. At that time adult children could be required to support an elderly parent who was poor and infirm, but the household means test forced them to support an out-of-work father who was neither elderly nor infirm.[75] The expectation was that the social obligation to share resources between household members would supplement any legal obligation, though sometimes the result could be the expulsion of the beneficiary from the home.

Thus, while the emphasis of the poor law administration in earlier times was on community provision, a shift towards prioritizing family support

---

[71] Primarily Income Support and Family Credit.

[72] Child Support Act 1995, Sch. 2, inserting new Sch. 4B into the Child Support Act 1991; the matters include designated "special expenses" (costs of travel to work, costs of maintaining contact, debts incurred for the benefit of the family by the parent before he left, benefits conferred on the beneficiary parent before the scheme came into effect by capital or property transfer).

[73] Thomson (1989: 58).

[74] Crowther (1982: 138).

[75] Crowther (1982: 142).

occurred during the nineteenth and early twentieth centuries, although much depended on local discretion. It was not until after the Second World War, with the introduction of the welfare state, that the balance moved decisively back to the community. Relatives were still under a legal obligation to contribute to the support of their impoverished kin, but the definition of liable relatives was narrowed by removing grandparents from this category and abolishing the obligation on adult children to support their elderly parents. In principle the state undertook to provide full subsistence to all who needed it, recouping a contribution from "liable relatives". But the social security authorities retained a wide discretion when recovering this money and their practice, described by the Finer Committee in 1974[76] reveals that this was seen as being of relatively minor significance. The proposals of the Committee itself for a "guaranteed maintenance allowance" for one-parent families, which were never implemented, were perhaps a high-water mark in post-war prioritization of communal over family support obligations.[77]

However in recent years the manipulation of indirect obligations in order to re-assert familial obligations has become an increasingly important feature of social policy. For example, the indirect obligation to support a child lasts until the child is 16, although it can be extended to 19 in certain circumstances.[78] But in an attempt to persuade children over 16 who had left school and did not have work into work training schemes, the Social Security Act 1988 raised the age of entitlement of a child to Income Support from 16 to 18 (with certain exceptions) and reduced the benefit levels for those between 18 and 25.[79] If they did not enter such a scheme, the Government relied upon parents complying with the social obligation it believed fell on them to support the children, although it was not a legal obligation. In 1985 the rights of unemployed teenagers who had left home to claim board and lodging allowances were restricted. "If they could not find a job", observes Hilary Land (1995: 196) "they were expected to move elsewhere or—preferably—to return home. Failure to do so resulted in their benefit being substantially cut or stopped altogether". Benefits for people under 25 were reduced on the assumption that they would be living at home (although only about a half of claimants at that age were doing so). In 1990/91 full-time students lost entitlement to Income Support, unemployment and housing benefits and the value of the student maintenance grant has been progressively eroded. Land (1995: 200) observes that "families are now expected to support their children throughout their teens and into their early twenties to a greater extent than ever before".

Since indirect obligations are enforced by a third party (in this case, the state), that party can enforce them in accordance with its own priorities.

[76] *Report of the Committee on One-Parent Families* (1974, Cmnd. 5629) vol. 1, paras. 4.184–9.

[77] Discussed by Maclean and Eekelaar (1993).

[78] Child Support Act 1991, s. 55.

[79] Ogus, Barendt and Wikeley (1995: 462); Morrow and Richards (1996: 7).

These may involve attempting to subordinate certain sets of obligations to others. For example, before the establishment of the Child Support Agency, when the social security authorities decided how much, if anything, an "absent father" should contribute to the state towards the costs of providing social security benefits for his children, they permitted him to retain sufficient income to allow him to fulfil his (assumed) social obligations towards his new family household members. The courts, on the other hand, when enforcing the obligation directly on the application of the mother, did not.[80] The Child Support Act 1991 reversed the previous social security policy, and no allowance is made, in calculating the absent parent's assessable income, for any social obligation he may be thought to be under to support a new adult partner or children of his new household, except natural children of his.[81] A minor amendment in 1995 allows an application to be made for modification of the assessment to take into account the costs of "supporting a child who is not (the debtor-parent's) child but who is part of his family". This however is confined to the support of stepchildren with respect to whom the absent parent undertook a social obligation before the Act came into effect, so the fundamental orientation of the scheme remains unchanged.[82]

Further examples can be found with respect to care and provision for the elderly. Although there is now no direct or indirect legal duty on children to support their parents, local authorities are using their discretionary powers to assess not only the means of spouses but also those of adult children when deciding whether to offer care to elderly persons.[83] Adult children may also be expected to forego an expected inheritance and accept the sale of their parents' property in order to finance the parents' care.[84]

In these cases it seems that the state can use its powers to expose at its discretion the web of social obligations which policy-makers believe forms the backdrop against which legal obligations are formulated. The result may be effectively to expand the defined limits of the legal obligations beyond the statutory time-limits, or to classes of individuals who fall outside the definitions, or to supplement them by obligations which are seen to arise by reason of sharing a household.

---

[80] *Report of the Committee on One-Parent Families*, (Cmnd 5629), paras. 4.203–4.205 (London, HMSO, 1974); Eekelaar (1976: 68).

[81] Bainham (1993: 310). Note that the "general principles" referred to in the new s. 28E (set out in note 59 above) do not require the officer to have regard to any obligation towards a member of a parent's *de facto* family.

[82] Child Support Act 1995, inserting new Sch. 4B into the Child Support Act 1991; Child Support Departure Directions (Anticipatory Application) Regulations 1996 (S.I. 1996 No 635), reg.18(2).

[83] See Millar and Warman (1996: 51, 56).

[84] For similar developments in New Zealand, see Peart (1996).

SHARING A HOUSEHOLD

The fact that people live in a common household may clearly affect their economic resources. They may share the rent, and would normally share the benefits of common services like electricity and water. Running one household is cheaper than running two at the equivalent standard. But does the fact alone that people share their resources in a common household lead to an obligation that they *should* do so;[85] in particular, does such an obligation continue if the household breaks up?

Direct obligations

It seems as if household sharing may play a part in generating obligations directly, but it is not sufficient in itself to do so. In this respect it is like marriage. For example, a spouse may be ordered to pay support for a child whom he or she has "treated" as a child of the family.[86] Where therefore a stepchild has lived in a household for a considerable time, that fact alone will be significant in constituting a support obligation for the stepparents.[87] But it will not be conclusive. First, the obligation will only arise if the stepparents are married to one another; secondly, account is taken of the obligations other people may have towards the child and also the extent to which the stepparent "assumed responsibility" for the child and indeed whether this was done knowing the child was or was not his own.[88]

Another example of the potential of household sharing to give rise to obligations is where households are shared by adults who are not married to each other. The law has in fact been very reluctant to recognize this, but there are signs of change. Someone who lives with another in a property owned by that other may acquire rights in the property, but this theoretically depends on the presence of additional elements, such as direct financial contribution to the acquisition of the property, or the presence of a common intention that one party was to have such rights, or where a court thinks that a transfer of property rights is justified as a result of inducement by the owner and reliance by the other.[89] Rights have sometimes even been given against third parties on the basis of household sharing, but again other factors need to be present. For example, the survivor of a couple who are living together as husband and wife (even if not married) may succeed to a protected private tenancy or a public

---

[85] Especially as some may not actually do so: see Wilson (1987).

[86] Matrimonial Causes Act 1973, s. 52(1).

[87] See *Carron* v. *Carron* [1984] FLR 805, where Ormrod LJ said: "You cannot live with children of this age (two and eight) for four years without treating them as children of the family".

[88] See the discussion in Barton and Douglas (1995: 230–1).

[89] These propositions refer to a complex web of law, the details of which have been the subject of much literature, but which are not relevant for present purposes.

sector tenancy that was in the name of the deceased.[90] Such a couple are also given special protection should one suffer violence at the hands of the other, though this is slightly weaker than the protection given to married couples,[91] and it is possible for the courts to transfer a tenancy from one partner to the other.[92] (Of course if the couple are, or have been, married, an obligation may arise (see p. 31 above)).

The fact that these provisions require the outward appearance of marriage imposes a superadded requirement to mere home-sharing.[93] But it is possible to obtain a non-molestation order against someone simply on the basis that the two people concerned "live or have lived in the same household, otherwise than merely by reason of one of them being the other's employee, tenant, lodger or boarder".[94] So a partner in a same-sex shared household can take advantage of that provision. The Law Commission is considering whether "home-sharing" might in itself form the basis for the acquisition of certain rights and duties.

Indirect obligations

The assumption that the social obligations which are thought to arise by sharing a common household will be discharged is made by modern social security law when it deprives an individual (usually a woman) who would otherwise qualify for Income Support of her benefits when he or she cohabits with another outside marriage. It does this by treating a "man and a woman who are not married to each other but are living as husband and wife" as if they were married and living in the same household.[95] Although they have no legal duty to support one another, it is assumed that they will respect an obligation of support raised by sharing a household. Not to do this would give the unmarried a significant advantage over the married, because in their case the social security authorities give indirect effect to the obligation to support which arises both from marriage and household sharing (see p. 32). This does not, however, occur where couples of the same sex share a home. In this context, then, it seems as if we are unwilling to encourage, or even assume, a social obligation of support arising entirely from the fact of sharing a household. In fact, it seems that in the case of indirect obligations as well as direct ones, a social obligation of support will not be perceived to arise from the fact

[90] Housing Act 1988, s. 87 and Sch. 4. *Dyson Holdings* v. *Fox* [1976] QB 503. See also Law Reform (Succession) Act 1995 allowing a person who had lived in the same household as the deceased and "as the husband or wife" of the deceased to make a claim against the estate.

[91] An order can be made excluding the property-owning partner from the home, but for a shorter time than if they were married: Family Law Act 1996, Part IV (see p. 144 below).

[92] Family Law Act 1996, Sch. 7.

[93] See *Harrogate Borough Council* v. *Simpson* [1986] 2 FLR 91.

[94] Family Law Act 1996, ss. 42, 62(3).

[95] Social Security Contributions and Benefits Act 1992, s. 137(1).

of home-sharing alone. But home-sharing, when accompanied by some other relationship, may create an indirectly enforced social obligation which would not occur were it not for the home-sharing.

CONCLUSIONS

This chapter has described the varieties of familial obligations by looking at those circumstances where the law has defined such obligations by distinguishing those which are directly enforceable from those which are implemented indirectly and by explaining their interaction with (assumed) social obligations. The emphasis has been on coercion; that is, the means by which pressure may be brought upon individuals to comply with these obligations. In one instance, however, where the Child Support Act 1991 declined to make an allowance for any social obligation a man might have towards his stepchildren and new partner with whom he is living when determining the support he must pay to his natural children, we can detect an attempt to undermine a possible social obligation. But, *once the father's income falls below a specified level* (the "protected income level"), then that social obligation is given limited recognition because, if that happens, the father's child support liability will be reduced if meeting it would reduce his income below a level which would enable him to fulfil his social obligation to support his *de facto* second family (including unmarried partner and stepchildren) at subsistence levels, notwithstanding that he has no *legal* obligation to do so at all.[96] If it did not do that, the state would need to support his *de facto* family directly. One might say, cynically, that the state is happy to rely on him exercising his assumed social obligation to support *de facto* household members if this will take the burden off the state (as in the "protected income" situation) but prefers to undercut the obligation if recognizing it would increase the burden on the state to support his first family.

[96] Child Support Act 1991, Sch. 1, para. 6.

4

Parenthood Across Households

The previous two chapters examined the broad social context of contemporary family living in the United Kingdom and the basis upon which the legal obligation of family members to support each other operated. In this final chapter before we set out our data, we look specifically at those situations where parenthood is stretched across two households. We are concerned here with the effects of this on the children. Children's familial experiences are important not only because they affect their psychological development but also because they are, or may be, a resource upon which they can draw. In their discussion of the effects of living in a one-parent family, Sara McLanahan and Gary Sandefur (1994) use the expression "social capital" to refer generally to the social resources available to the children of those families. The term is derived from G. Loury through the sociologist James Coleman (1990: 306) who defines it as "a set of resources that inhere in family relations and in community social organization and that are useful for the cognitive or social development of the child".

Like McLanahan and Sandefur, we see social capital as comprising mainly the set of relationships of commitment and trust on which the child can call from the time of its birth, though we would include the material resources which tend to be associated with access to those relationships. When, therefore, children's parents live apart, their value as a resource for children may be damaged, or at least altered in some way. This chapter therefore looks at what some of the research evidence tells us about the way disruption of the parental relationship affects its potential to provide social capital for children.

We need to consider first the way the law structures cross-household parenthood, and then current opinions as to its effects on the children concerned.

THE LEGAL POSITION OF THE OUTSIDE PARENT

The issue of the relationship between a child and a parent who is living outside the household has only recently been seen to raise a problem for the child. In the past, it was dominated by two overriding motifs: the father's rights as guardian, and moral judgement (in particular of the mother). If the child was born within marriage, the father, not the mother, was the natural guardian and was accordingly entitled to keep the child (though how often he did so is unclear). The Custody of Infants Act 1839 permitted the Lord Chancellor or Master of the Rolls to allow a mother who had not committed adultery access to her children if they were with the father and even to grant her "legal custody" if the child was under 7. In 1873 the age was extended to 16 and the adultery bar lifted.[1]

Clearly, the mother who was granted legal custody acquired whatever legal rights were necessary to bring up the child she was looking after,[2] but mothers remained in a secondary position to fathers because they needed a court order to protect their relationship with the child, and to obtain this they needed to separate from the father (which might be impractical) and to avoid the moral disapproval of the court. Furthermore, if the mother did not receive legal custody and the child stayed with the father, all she could hope for was to be allowed "access" to the child; she had no further "rights". Extensive campaigns by women's groups for equalizing parental rights in the late nineteenth and early twentieth centuries failed at the hands of male perceptions that family unity required a single "family head" and that legal intrusion would introduce disharmony into families.[3] Equality of rights between married parents was achieved only in 1973.[4]

The fact that a married mother now had the same rights with respect to her child as the father had did not, however, resolve the question as to what rights were held by the outside parent after divorce or separation. Commonly, on divorce, "sole custody" was granted to one of the parents (usually the mother).[5] In theory, this did not affect the "rights" of the other parent, although it might be difficult to exercise them.[6] However, the practice adopted by some judges in the 1970s of making "joint custody" orders[7] created confusion. Did this mean that such an order was now necessary in order to retain the outside parent's "rights"? If not, what was its purpose? Judicial opinion was divided,[8] and the problem was resolved when the Children Act 1989 abolished the concept of "custody", replacing it with "parental responsibility". Under that Act, each parent retains parental responsibility, even after divorce. This idea, too, has caused difficulty, but, as has been explained earlier (p. 37), it seems to mean no more than that either parent can legitimately carry out parental functions insofar as they can practicably do so; it gives neither a

---

[1] Custody of Infants Act 1873. See also Summary Jurisdiction (etc) Act 1895.

[2] See Eekelaar (1973: 230) for a full discussion.

[3] See Brophy (1982); Maidment (1984).

[4] Guardianship Act 1973, s. 1.

[5] In the 1970s it was found in England and Wales and in Scotland that custody was granted to the mother in three-quarters of cases: Eekelaar and Clive (1977), Table 34.

[6] See *Re T*. [1963] Ch. 238 (absent father retains rights concerning child's name); *Dipper* v. *Dipper* [1980] 2 All ER 722 at 731.

[7] The practice was not widespread: in 1977 it was found in only 3.4% of cases in England and Wales, and none in Scotland: Eekelaar and Clive (1977), Table 34.

[8] Compare *Dipper* v. *Dipper*, above, with *Jussa* v. *Jussa* [1972] 2 All ER 600; Priest and Whybrow (1986: 51–2).

better right than the other to take any decision regarding the child, and the parents are under no duty to consult one another before taking a decision.

One obvious right which an outside parent would seem to have is to visit the child. There never seems to have been difficulty in allowing this to divorced fathers (whatever their moral standing), either because they retained their "natural guardianship" (and this would seem to include a "right" to visit the child), or because they seldom sought to exercise it. However for many years courts refused to allow an adulterous mother to visit her children (remember that she was not the child's "natural guardian".)[9] This attitude persisted until 1924.[10] As recently as in 1962 a judge refused a mother access to her children because on one occasion she had failed to return home at night, leaving the children with the husband, and sometimes the children had not changed from their night-clothes by 11.30 a.m.![11] But the Court of Appeal overturned the decision, saying that the right to visit was "no more than the basic right of any parent", to be forfeited only in very serious circumstances.

Although in 1973 the "right" of "access" was re-characterized as being "the right of the child" rather than of the parent,[12] extraordinarily little attention was paid to the relationship between children and the parent from whom they had become separated. When custody was "awarded" to the one parent, courts often expressly granted "reasonable access" to the other, but this seems to have been a perfunctory declaration and was done in only about half of cases, practice varying between courts.[13] The fact that provision for access had not been expressly made did not prevent its exercise, and it was very rare for access to be specifically prohibited. One can conclude that in the overwhelming majority of cases the matter was left to the parents to arrange as they wished. Research in the 1970s suggested that in about one-third of divorces involving children contact with the separated parent stopped altogether.[14]

THE DESIRABILITY OF CONTACT

The emergence of a new orthodoxy

During the 1970s it seemed that a large proportion of children, growing as the divorce rate climbed, were being deprived of contact with one parent. Opinion was divided over the extent to which this might be harmful to the children. In the years immediately following the Second World War, John Bowlby

---

[9] *Seddon* v. *Seddon* (1862) 2 Sw. & Tr. 642.
[10] *B.* v. *B.* [1924] P 176.
[11] *S* v. *S* [1962] 2 All ER 1.
[12] *M.* v. *M.* [1973] 2 All ER 81.
[13] Eekelaar and Clive (1977: 20–2).
[14] Eekelaar (1984: 68).

(1951), (1969) had propounded the view, based on a variety of research studies, many involving children who had been separated from their parents and been brought up in residential settings, that disruption of the bond between mother and child, even at very early ages, caused potentially irreparable psychological harm to children. This gave rise to speculation that being in a broken home might itself cause behavioural disturbances in children. However, this view was firmly dismissed by Michael Rutter (1972), who argued that other research showed that behavioural problems in children were associated with the presence of conflict between their parents, not whether or not the home was broken. Bowlby's views were also criticized as being based on flawed research (especially that the conditions of the children observed were more likely to be caused by their poor care after separation from their mothers) and to be serving a political agenda which wished to re-establish women's place within the home in a period of excess labour as a result of demobilization.[15]

In 1973, in a controversial book, Joseph Goldstein, Anna Freud and Albert Solnit (1973) drew together both the continuity and the conflict theories. They proclaimed (on the basis of "psychoanalytic theory") the "need of every child for unbroken continuity of affectionate and stimulating relationships with an adult", whom they called the child's "psychological parent". They believed that when parents separated, the child could sustain that relationship properly with only one parent and that the continuity of this relationship was threatened by "provid(ing) the noncustodial parent with the right to visit or forc(ing) the child to visit". If such visits were to occur, that should be entirely at the discretion of the custodial parent. In a postscript in 1979, the authors explained that they were not opposed to such contacts (although they expressed scepticism about their value) and indeed believed that, other things being equal, courts might prefer to give custody to the parent most willing to allow them, but retained their view that "the custodial parent should be free" to reject them.

The implications of Goldstein, Freud and Solnit's position for the outside parent are bleak, for they give ultimate control over the post-separation arrangement to the person caring for the child. In order to bolster the child's "trust" of the psychological parent, that parent is given a free hand to determine the child's interests on this matter, in much the same way as nineteenth century courts felt it was in the child's interests to be controlled by its father.[16] A further issue was raised by the critics of Goldstein, Freud and Solnit: to give the parent with the child the sole power to determine its relationship with the other parent creates an imbalance in power between the parents which could have seriously adverse consequences on other aspects of their post-divorce

[15] See Clarke and Clarke (1976); Brophy (1982).
[16] Goldstein, Freud and Solnit also ignore the likelihood that their position would encourage litigation of custody by men fearful that losing possession of the child could sever the relationship completely: Strauss and Strauss (1974); Eekelaar (1984: 83–4).

relationship. In fact, the political climate was moving against the authors' position. In the 1970s (primarily) men's groups, such as the Campaign for Justice in Divorce and Families Need Fathers were formed to resist what they perceived to be the unfavourable treatment by the law of divorced men, both as regards financial support obligations and custody and visitation issues. In England and Wales the campaigns bore partial fruit in the provisions of the Matrimonial and Family Proceedings Act 1984 which encouraged the idea of financial self-sufficiency after divorce and in the concept of the Children Act 1989 that joint parental responsibility survives the parents' divorce. In the USA, most states followed California's lead in 1979 and in the 1980s passed statutes which allowed or encouraged "joint custody".[17] The English courts more recently appear to be acting on the principle that the involvement of the "outside" parent in the child's life must be assumed to be beneficial for the child unless it is clearly demonstrated not to be.[18] The Family Law Act 1996 expressly enacts that in divorce proceedings in which children are involved the court must consider whether to exercise any of its powers under the Children Act 1989, and, if it considers that the circumstances are such as to require it, or are likely to require it, to exercise those powers, it must "have particular regard, on the evidence before it, to . . . the general principle that, in the absence of evidence to the contrary, the welfare of the child will be best served by (i) his having regular contact with those who have parental responsibility for him and with other members of his family; and (ii) the maintenance of as good a continuing relationship with his parents as is possible".[19]

It is not surprising that some feminist writers have detected a patriarchal agenda whereby separated fathers are attempting to retain power "not simply over their children, but also, through the children, over their wives".[20] There is indeed evidence that some fathers use contact as a means to continue to inflict violence on mothers and children.[21] It is also argued that, by identifying contact between a child and its separated father as being good for the child, women who do not wish to co-operate with the absent father are being characterized as selfish and bad mothers.[22] Such moral critiques are characteristic responses of those in authority when confronted by individuals who deviate from orthodoxy. How far, then, can the new orthodoxy be supported on grounds independent from the "mere" desire of fathers to have a say in the upbringing of their children?

---

[17] Maccoby and Mnookin (1992: 9); Emery (1994: 76–9).
[18] *Re H (Minors) (Access)* [1992] 1 FLR 148.
[19] Family Law Act 1996, s. 11(2), (4).
[20] Brophy (1982: 150).
[21] Hester and Radford (1996).
[22] Smart (1989: 10).

Research evidence[23]

Rutter's theory that conflict was worse than separation for children suggests that parental contact after divorce might sometimes be detrimental to children, and Goldstein, Freud and Solnit (1973) support that interpretation. However, in an important paper, Martin Richards (1987) sought to limit the scope of Rutter's observations. He noted that Rutter's argument was "very specific". It related only to boys and was restricted to delinquency outcomes, not other harms. Furthermore, Rutter had compared conflicted cases with separations caused by death of a parent. This overlooked a variety of features which seemed to be present when living parents separated; for example, the potential loss by the child of relationships with the kin-group of the outside parent, the financial and other difficulties facing the one-parent family and potential conflicts inherent in reconstituting the family. In 1994 Richards used language very reminiscent of Bowlby's attachment theory itself: "The evidence suggests that it is the breaking of already existing relationships which has ill effects for children".[24]

Reviewing the literature on the effects of divorce, Amato and Keith (1991) observed that the effects of divorce tended to be measured according to three main factors: economic deprivation, family structures and psychological stress. The first type of study noted the adverse consequences which the economic effects of divorce had on children, though these would usually be shared with children in other types of one-parent family. The second focused on the effects which disruption of family relationships had on children, and the third concentrated on the effects of inter-parental conflict. Although all three factors can affect each other, the last two seem particularly close, and we think it might be more convenient to distinguish between relational and structural factors associated with parental absence. The former concern the effects on a child's personal well-being emanating mostly from disturbances in the child's own inter-personal relationships and in those around the child. The latter concern the effects which parental absence has on the family's place in the social environment, and which in turn have consequences for the children of the family.[25]

Relational factors

A number of studies seem to show that it is not the fact of divorce, or separation, which is important for the child's well-being, but what Hess and Camara (1979) called "family processes", that is, the communication between the parents and their interest in and closeness to the children. Their research

---

[23] For a useful and accessible recent review of the research evidence, see Pryor and Seymour (1996).

[24] Richards (1994: 309).

[25] For a similar analysis, see Eekelaar (1991: 45).

indicated that, after divorce, the quality of the parents' affective relationship with the child was more important than their own relationship.[26] Theirs was a small study of 32 white middle-class families (half divorced, half intact). A larger sample of 184 divorcing families in the San Francisco Bay Area, reported in 1991, showed similar results. While conflict between parents appeared to have indirect (through impaired parent-child relationships) and direct effects on children's behaviour after divorce, emotional adjustment was related neither to the extent of post-parental conflict nor to the extent of contact with the father. The most important influence seemed to be the degree of conflict *during the marriage*.[27] However, some other American studies have shown that young adolescents from divorced families where high levels of inter-parental conflict continued after divorce were less well adjusted than adolescents whose divorced parents reduced their conflict after divorce[28] and that it is that conflict in itself, as much as the children's awareness of it, "probably through disrupting parenting, (which) is the primary mechanism of difficulty in adolescent competence. However, by examining adolescents and how they perceive and probably cope with the situation, a small but significant piece is added to the puzzle of understanding adolescent functioning".[29]

In 1991 a British study drawn from the National Child Development Survey, a sample constituted from all children born in the first week of March 1958, revealed that "impaired" behaviour (measured in terms of disruptive behaviour, being unhappy and worried, reading ability and mathematical ability) of children whose parents had divorced was present *before* the divorce. Children of divorced parents scored worse scores than children whose parents remained together well before their parents divorced as well as afterwards.[30] The following year the same conclusions were reached when American data were added to the British.[31] It appears, therefore, that while many of the problems manifested by children after divorce have their origins in the circumstances of the marriage, these may be aggravated by continued inter-parental conflict after divorce.

Hess and Camara (1979) are sometimes cited as demonstrating that keeping contact with an absent parent is beneficial. However, all they show is that

---

[26] For similar results, also from a small study, which showed that experiences *prior to* divorce were stronger than the effect of divorce itself, see Block, Block and Gjerde (1986).

[27] Kline, Johnston and Tschann (1991).

[28] Long, Slater, Forehand and Fauber (1988) (sample of 35 white adolescents aged 11–15). Long, Forehand, Fauber and Brody (1987) (sample of 40 white adolescents aged 11–15) also found that independent assessment of these children's competence related their dysfunctional behaviour to post-divorce parental conflict.

[29] Wierson, Forehand and McCombs (1988: 717) (sample of 178 subjects aged 10–15). Contrast a report of research claiming that high achieving children were "more likely" to come from conflicted families with a strong sense of cohesion (which was helped by one parent being absent for part of childhood): *The Times*, 18 December 1996, 6.

[30] Elliott and Richards (1991).

[31] Cherlin, Furstenberg, Chase-Landsdale, Kiernan, Robins, Morison and Teitler (1992).

children with good relationships with both parents do best, those with "negative" relationships with both do worst, and those with a good relationship with one and a "negative" relationship with another, come in between. They found frequency of contact to be irrelevant. In any case, the quality of these relationships could reflect the position prior to the divorce, which seems to be the most important factor. In 1987 Furstenberg, Morgan and Allison (1987) drew a sample of 227 children who were living with their mothers only after divorce and whose fathers were alive, from a panel of 1,423 children (the US National Survey of Children). They adjudged the children's "well-being" from reports by mothers, teachers and the children themselves on matters such as delinquency, problem behaviour, distress and academic performance. They found no support for the hypothesis that paternal contact was beneficial to the children. Indeed, those who had not seen the father for five years did significantly better than those who had spent up to thirteen days with him over the previous year.[32] The child's sex, and the mother's marital status made no difference. Nor did children seem to do better when they "felt closer" to the father. However, failure by the father to contribute financially was associated with negative behaviour. In a later study from a sample of highly conflicted families referred for counselling, greater access was associated with more disturbance in the children.[33]

On the other hand, a study by Camara and Resnick (1989) based on 82 families living in the Boston area with children aged 7 to 9 measured the observed behaviour of the children against the strategies used by both divorced and still-married parents for dealing with their disputes. The strategies were broken down into "verbal attack", "avoidance", "compromise" and "physical anger". It was found that "strategies used by parents to manage conflict which involved verbal attack or physically violent behaviour towards the other parent were associated with poorer child adjustment . . . Those divorced parents who co-operated with each other around issues of visitation, discipline, family routines and celebrations, and in meeting the children's developmental needs, and who used negotiation and compromise when disagreements did occur, were more likely to have children who were more affiliative in play with other children, who engage in more positive play behaviour with other children, and who had higher self-esteem". It may be expected that children who observe aggressive behaviour in their parents are more likely to show anti-social traits in their own inter-personal dealings than those whose parents behave in more accommodating ways. What has not been established is whether a child whose separated parents behave gently and reasonably to her and to one another, but who sees the outside parent rarely or never, somehow does "less well" than a child of similar parents who sees the outside parent often. The well-known publications by Wallerstein and Kelly (1980) and

---

[32] See also Kline, Johnston and Tschann (1991).
[33] Johnston, Kline and Tschann (1989); see also Buchanan, Maccoby and Dornbusch (1991), for similar findings.

Wallerstein and Blakeslee (1989), which describe the psychological difficulties of children whose parents divorced, draw on the experiences of 60 families who sought counselling, and do not provide a reliable basis for generalisation about the effects of divorce on children.

Healy and others (1990) remarked on the ambiguity of the evidence concerning the effects of contact between children and an outside parent, and emphasized that "the child's relationship with a non-custodial father does not have simple, direct effects; rather, it has different implications for different kinds of children and for children in different situations". Their own study of 121 children aged between 6 and 12 whose parents recently separated showed that within the first eight months from the separation frequent and regular visits had most positive effects on the self-esteem of boys aged 6 to 8 but for older children and for girls they lowered their self-esteem (without adversely affected their behaviour), but that one year later visit frequency was associated with fewer problems for older children. Regularity of visits rather than their frequency was important if they were to be beneficial. In view of the variety of variables, it is not surprising that Robert Emery (1994: 211) concluded that "great caution must be exercised about drawing conclusions about children's relationships with their nonresidential parents when so much has gone unmeasured in research to date".

What is the effect on children of new relationships entered into by the parent looking after them? Clearly difficulties can arise within stepfamilies, and small-scale American studies have shown that much depends on the circumstances, including the age and the sex of the children.[34] Elliott and Richards' (1991) large-scale British study showed that remarriage by the mother had no positive or negative effects on the children's educational attainments.[35] It did, however, cause greater disruptive behaviour and more unhappiness and worry, but not to any large degree.

Elsa Ferri (1984) reported on the British National Child Development Study data which showed that children in stepfamilies were thought by their parents to manifest more problem behaviour than children who were with their natural parents, though this was not confirmed by teachers. Indeed, there were no significant behavioural differences between children living in a stepfamily and those living in a one-parent family, although the study showed that remarried families were "considerably" better off financially than one-parent families. Ferri (1984: 117) concluded that "for the majority of children we studied there was no discernible adverse effect (of remarriage) and little to distinguish them from their peers living with two natural parents. Yet, there was sufficient indication of unhappiness and developmental difficulties among a minority of stepchildren to suggest that remarriage should not be seen as an instant all-purpose 'cure' for the many problems faced by the one-parent family, especially if those problems are viewed from the child's perspectives". In

[34] See Hetherington (1989).
[35] Similarly for the USA: see McLanahan and Sandefur (1994: 70).

short, while remarriage may not *overcome* the relational ill-effects of a previous breakdown, there was no evidence that it made them any worse.

Spruijt and de Goede (1996) report a Dutch study which compared the well-being of adolescents from stable and conflicted intact families with that of adolescents in a one-parent family and in a stepfamily after divorce. Well-being comprised physical and psychological health, "relational well-being" (experience of relationships with others) and their employment situation. This found that children from the stable intact families had the best general results and those in the one-parent families the worst. The other two groups fell between them. Those from conflicted intact families were close to those from one-parent families (the "worst" group) in terms of physical and psychological well-being, but closer to stable intact families (the "best" group) with respect to their emotional relationships and employment situation. This suggests that intra-familial conflict causes disturbance, which may extend beyond the breakup of the family, but also that remaining in an intact family, even if conflicted, helps with employment prospects. As for the children moving into stepfamilies, these were closer to the stable intact (the "best") group as far as physical, relational and occupational matters were concerned, but closer to the one-parent (the "worst") group on psychological matters.[36] In their case, reconstitution seems to help them in many respects, but they may retain psychological problems, either from the experience of reconstitution or from the original conflict.

Structural factors

The findings in the Dutch study that employment prospects were better for children in intact or reconstituted families raises the question how far living in a one-parent family *in itself* jeopardises children's social capital. There is a good deal of evidence that it does. This has been extensively analysed in the American context by McLanahan and Sandefur (1994). They point out (1994: 23) that "single-mother families have had higher poverty rates than other families for as far back as we have data on poverty and family income". This suggests a structural explanation. It is not hard to find. Most one-parent families are headed by the mother. Women's incomes are in any event lower than those of men, and mothers with children are likely to find it even harder to sustain high-paid employment.[37] Even if the father's income was available to them, the family lacks the economies of scale which would be available if it were intact. In any case, support payments by outside fathers, if paid at all, tend to form a small portion of a family's income. If the parents had

---

[36] Similarly in the USA, survey data show that children in stepfamilies are similar to those in mother-only homes as far as psychological health is concerned: see Furstenberg and Cherlin (1991: 89).

[37] In 1994, 48% of women without dependent children worked full-time and 22% part-time compared to 23% with dependent children who worked full-time and 37% part-time: *General Household Survey 1994*, Table 7.7.

previously been married, the father's economic status invariably improves after divorce, while that of the mother who is looking after the children declines.[38] In addition to the disadvantages created by relative poverty, children in one-parent families experience loss of social capital either through disruption of relationships with the father's kinship network[39] or with wider community resources. American evidence shows that children of divorced and separated parents move more often than children of intact families, and a separation may cause other dislocations in the children's social networks (such as schooling).[40]

The consequences of these structural features appear in lower educational attainments, less employment participation and earlier entry into new families. McLanahan and Sandefur demonstrate this by reference to high-school drop-out rates, which are twice as high for children of one-parent families as for children from intact families. Their school performance, educational expectations and enrolment in further education are also lower. Even if the children of one-parent families finished high-school, their chances of being out-of-work was higher than for those from two-parent homes. Finally, all data sets show a higher risk of teenage birth for girls from one-parent homes from an increased risk of 5 percentage points to 17 percentage points.

In Britain, the Medical Research Council's National Survey of Health and Development allowed a follow-up study of all children born between 3 and 9 March 1946 when they reached the age of 36. Maclean and Wadsworth (1988) showed from this data that by the age of 36, people whose parents had divorced before they were 16 were more likely than others to be unemployed and seeking work (9.4 as against 4.2 per cent); less likely to be employed (83.3 as against 94.1 per cent) and to have lower weekly earnings (24.3 per cent over £160, as against 34.7 per cent).[41] Kiernan (1996), using data from the National Child Development Study, focused on whether a child's mother had been in employment or not, and found that this seemed to have an important effect on the child later position in life. She found that when they were 16, both boys and girls from intact families had higher qualifications than the others, but within the lone-mother families, *girls whose mothers had been unemployed* were much more likely to have had no educational qualifications and much less likely to have higher qualifications than those whose mothers had been employed. This did not hold, however, for the boys. By the time they were 33, women brought up by lone mothers who had been employed had a similar income and household status to those who had been in intact families, but those brought up by non-working lone mothers were much more likely to

---

[38] McLanahan and Sandefur (1994: 25) (reviewing American evidence). Our previous research demonstrated the same position in the United Kingdom: Eekelaar and Maclean (1986). For data from this study, see pp. 29–30.

[39] Richards (1994).

[40] McLanahan and Sandefur (1994: 32).

[41] Maclean and Wadsworth (1988).

have low levels of household income, to be living on income support and to be in rented accommodation than the rest. Men, too, from non-employed lone mother families were more likely to be unemployed at 33 and to be less well off than the rest. However, the differences tended to be stronger for females than for males. Whatever the reasons for these apparent differences, they suggest that a mother's employment status, especially if she is a lone parent, affects a child's social capital. They therefore have relevance for our data about the employment patterns of mothers which we set out later.

Having considered the state of knowledge on the effects of divorce and of cross-household parenting on children provided by current research, it is now time to present the evidence of our own study. This is deployed in the following three chapters. It will be seen that this does not always address exactly the same questions as the research which has been discussed. However, it does raise some important new questions against which current knowledge should be viewed.

5

Children Who Never Lived with Both Parents Together

Research on the effects of the experience of living in a one-parent family is usually either restricted to children who have experienced the divorce of their parents or focuses on children currently in one-parent families irrespective of how the family came into being; for example, whether the parents had divorced, or had never married. Children who had been in a one-parent family, but whose parents subsequently repartnered, are often excluded. Of course there is much which such families do share in common; in particular, lower financial status than two-parent families. But such broad overviews fail to pick up the complexity of familial experiences over time of many of the children. We know relatively little about parental relationships which are not marked by some visible event: be it marriage or divorce. We need to probe beneath the formalities and outward appearance of things to obtain a richer picture of the children's experiences.

In order to obtain some understanding of the social capital available to the children of our study, we attempted to disaggregate the variety of familial contexts in which they were nurtured. A detailed description of the sample we used is given in the Appendix. Here we need say no more than that in the summer of 1994 we screened out from the general population a group of 249 parents who were not living with the other parent of the "study" child. The "study" child was a child living with one parent whose other parent was living outside the household. If more than one child in the household fell into that category, one child was randomly selected.

188 women and 61 men were interviewed. Of these 249 parents, forty-six (42 women and 4 men) had never lived with the other parent together with the "study" child. This proportion (18 per cent) is close to the proportion (15 per cent) of children born to mothers in the general population in England and Wales who do not share an address with the father (see p. 20). A further 51 parents had lived with but never married the other parent, a proportion (20 per cent) almost identical to the 19 per cent of children born to apparently unmarried cohabiting couples in 1994. The rest (152) had been married to the other parent. Again this proportion (62 per cent) is comparable to the proportion of all children born to married couples in 1994 (68 per cent) (see p. 20).

Early in 1997, Alan Marsh, Reuben Ford and Louise Finlayson (1997) published the fourth report of the Programme of Research into Low Income Families undertaken by the Department of Social Security and the Policy Studies Institute. The data reported is an analysis of the family circumstances of 880 *lone parents*, whereas our population was not confined to parents who were currently living alone. Nevertheless, Marsh, Ford and Finlayson do sometimes differentiate between lone parents who had never partnered, those who had separated from cohabitation and those who had separated from marriage or had been divorced. These are similar (but not identical) to our three categories. Despite certain differences between our data sets, we have thought it useful to make comparisons between the findings where this seemed relevant.

In this chapter we describe the familial circumstances experienced by the "study" child in the forty-six cases where the parents and child had never all lived together. We considered calling these children "one-parent children", but in the light of the data which emerged as described below, we rejected this idea because it gives a misleading impression of the relationships experienced by many of these children. Instead we have used the expression "never-together" to describe the group. The term refers to the *children*, not the parents, and represents the fact that the children had never lived together with both of their parents at the same time. In this respect it differs from Marsh, Ford and Finlayson's category of "never-partnered" lone parents, for, as we will see, some of the parents in our "never-together" category had indeed lived with the child's other parent; but the two had not lived together with the child at the same time.[1]

CHARACTERISTICS OF THIS GROUP

Our information came from forty-two mothers (who were looking after the child) and four fathers (who were the "outside" parent). We have pooled the information together where we could, but sometimes have sufficient information only from the forty-two mothers.

As we will see (p. 108), the mothers in this group were younger than those in the other two categories of the study, as is to be expected because the women in those categories had all experienced a period of unmarried or married cohabitation. Two-thirds of the parents of the 'never-together' group were under 30. Seventeen out of forty-two (41 per cent) were under 25, nearly one-third were in their thirties and only two over 40. Most had had the "study" child when they were under 25 (Table 5.1), whereas we have seen that, after 1992, although most women had their first child in their late

---

[1] Similarly, Marsh, Ford and Finlayson sometimes distinguish relations between the respondent lone parent and their first and subsequent partners (if there were any). We, however, were only concerned with the *parents* of the study child.

Table 5.1 Age of Mother at Birth of Study Child—
Never-together Group (n = 42)

Age	%
Under 20	32
20—24	39
25—29	15
30—35	7
Over 35	5

twenties, those who do not are more likely to have their first child in their thirties than in their early twenties (p. 18).

As we observed, some mothers had been married. Four had been married to the child's father but were divorced from him before the child was born and two had lived unmarried with the father but separated from him before the child was born. Two had divorced a man who was not the study child's father. These mothers were older; two were in their forties, and the rest in their thirties. If this group is removed, the age profile of the mothers who had not lived with the child's father drops still further. One mother was living with another man, not the father, when the child was born and was still living with him at the time of interview.

Consistently with this, there were proportionately many more children of young ages than would be found in a standard cross-section of the child population. Half of the children in this group were under 5, whereas only about a third of the total child population under 16 is under that age.[2] This is consistent with the fact that mothers who are not living at the same address as the fathers of their children tend to be younger than those living at the same address.[3] But why did we not find more older women who had borne a child some years ago by a man with whom they had never shared a home? Three possible explanations may be offered. The sample may be skewed by a lower participation rate by mothers with older children, though we did not find this for the other categories in our sample. Another might lie in the fact that many more children have been born into this category in recent years than there were 10 or more years ago (Haskey (1996c: 11)), and that this has led to the higher proportion of younger children in this segment of our sample. Another possibility is that a number of mothers who are living apart from the father when the child is born may cohabit with the fathers later, so they do not appear in this group when the children are older. This is more likely to have

[2] In 1994, 7% of the population in Great Britain was under 5 and 15% was aged from 5 to 15: *General Household Survey*, 1994. Table 2.28.
[3] See Burghes with Brown (1995: 17).

happened in the case of births occurring longer ago than the more recent births. Since such cases fell outside our study, we do not know whether this does happen and if so how frequently. However, we draw attention to the possibility of this particular variant of family formation.

Family relationships

When the children were born, in nearly half (twenty-one out of forty-six: 46 per cent) of the cases the mother was living with *her* family of origin.[4] This is consistent with the finding by Bradshaw and Millar (1991) that 58 per cent of single mothers were living with their parents prior to giving birth.[5] These children, at least initially, could draw support from their grandparents and possibly their mother's siblings. In three cases the mother was living with someone other than the father when the child was born (in one case earlier partner of hers). So in half of these cases the social capital available to the child in its immediate household extended beyond one adult. The enhanced role of maternal grandparents in cases of divorce has been noted in the USA by Cherlin and Furstenberg (1992: Ch. 6), and it seems that maternal grandparents may also play an important role for many children who have never lived in the same house as their father. Paternal grandparents may also have had some influence (see pp. 64–5). Other siblings were present in half of the remaining cases where the mother was the only adult, but in the rest there were none.

What, then, of the fathers? To what extent could they contribute to this capital? Looking at their circumstances at the time of the child's birth, we divided them into four classes, two determined on the basis of their relationships with an adult partner and two by the type of household in which they were living. Six out of forty-six (13 per cent) of the fathers were either married to or living "as married" with a woman other than the mother when the study child was born. We call these the "already partnered fathers". Another six out of forty-six (13 per cent) of the fathers, whom we will call the "divorced/separated fathers", had been married to, or had been living with, the mother before the study child was born, but had left her by the time of the birth. Just over one-third of the fathers (seventeen out of forty-six: 37 per cent) were known to be living at the home of their parents when the children were born (the "at home fathers"). Fifteen out of forty-six (33 per cent) were living independently of their parents ("independent fathers"), though two

[4] Burghes with Brown (1995: 18).
[5] Burghes with Brown (1995: 18). Similarly, Ermisch, Di Salvo and Joshi (1996: 13), using the 1958 National Child Development Study data, found that half of single mothers were living with their parents six months after the birth of the child.

were known to be living with relatives. Our respondents did not know the household status of two others.

Following the child's birth, three further groups had emerged by the time of interview. One comprised those who later formed a partnership with one or more women other than the mother. We considered that "partnering" occurred when a couple had lived together for more than six months. Since most of the men had not been in a partnership before, we call these "subsequently partnered fathers". Since a number of our respondents knew either little or nothing about the later relationships of the father there is an element of uncertainty in our information about how many in total fell into this class, but we had information that twelve out of forty-six (26 per cent) of them had subsequently partnered, with one having later separated. (We do not include in this category the two of those who were married to or cohabiting with another woman when the child was born but who were living with a different woman at the time of interview). A further group of twelve out of forty-six (26 per cent) of the fathers were known still to be living at their parents' home at the time of the interview and the remainder were not.[6]

We had some information on other children the men had fathered, but in the nature of things this information was incomplete, and we could not use this as an analytic group. We know that three of the fathers had children by other women prior to the birth of the study child and seven had children after its birth. One of these was a merchant seaman who had four separate families with children born both before and after the study child. We can therefore say little about the extent to which the fathers in this group were procreating children by various mothers without forming steady relationships, except that the group does not appear to be large. However, six out of forty-six (13 per cent) of the fathers had another child *by the mother of the study child* after that child's birth and while they were still not living with each other. These were, therefore, clearly ongoing relationships, types of family-formation without a common household.

These descriptions show the heterogeneity of familial experiences of this group of children. Some of them lost a potential resident biological father before birth through separation or divorce; two others gained a stepparent before their birth (another appeared to have one in readiness at the time of conception)! In a few cases the father remained embedded in a different, pre-existing family unit. But nearly half were born into a household comprising the mother's family of origin. At the time of the birth, in nearly two out of three cases the mothers were in touch with the fathers, so there was a possibility of access to and some level of financial and emotional support from the other parent and some form of cross-household parenting existed (though we will see that in many cases this failed to develop). Furthermore, the fact that

---

[6] Marsh, Ford and Finlayson (1997: Table 2.4) give 21 per cent of former "partners" of never-partnered lone parents as having subsequently partnered, and 15 per cent to be living with their own parents: but information was missing in half the cases.

more than one-third of the fathers were known to be living at home with their parents opens up possibilities for further familial contact and social capital. We will now examine these issues in more detail.

Resources available at the time of birth

Of the mothers living with their own parents when the baby was born (twenty-one out of forty-six: 46 per cent), the majority were in housing rented from the local authority or a housing association. Of the rest, only fifteen out of forty-six (33 per cent) were in accommodation held even in part in their own name; ten of these were renting and one was in bed and breakfast accommodation. Others were sharing houses with other people. Only four were in the owner-occupied sector, two of whom were in the older, divorced, group. Incomes were low and largely consisted of state benefits. Only three out of forty-two (7 per cent) of the mothers were employed and receiving some form of wage or maternity allowance when the baby was born. The rest (93 per cent) reported benefit payments as being their main source of income.

Not surprisingly, then, incomes were low. We do not have clear individual income data for mothers who formed part of a larger household, but in the case of those living independently (n = 23), the gross household income (net of tax) of a couple of them exceeded £6,000 a year, but it was under £4,000 for 52 per cent and between £4,000 and £6,000 for 35 per cent.[7] Given the mothers' educational qualifications, this is surprising because, although 40 per cent had no qualifications at all, 47 per cent had a GCE or GCSE, 2 per cent a vocational qualification, 2 per cent an A level and 9 per cent some kind of diploma or degree, and might be expected to find employment. The spread of qualifications for this group in our sample is, however, consistent with that given for single lone mothers in the *General Household Survey 1993*.[8] One was supported by relatives. But it does underline the difficulties which these mothers apparently have in finding, or possibly being able to cope with, employment. Even though nearly half were living with their parents, it seems this may not be sufficient to provide the child-care back-up which would facilitate employment. For example, their mothers might be in paid work themselves.

The fathers, too, were heavily reliant on benefits, but to nothing like the same extent as the mothers. Only twenty-one out of forty-six (46 per cent) were known to be in employment when the child was born. Fourteen were known to be on benefit, and we had no clear information from the mothers on the rest.

---

[7] This is consistent with the *General Household Survey* which for 1994 gave the weekly gross incomes of 57% of single lone mothers as being under £100 and of 15% as being between £100 and £150: *General Household Survey 1994*, Table 2.20. The GHS single lone mother category is not identical to the mothers in our "never-together" group, but is the closest to them of the national data sets.

[8] Table 2.27.

The picture revealed thus far of the children's position at birth has consistencies with the stereotype of young lone mothers, largely dependent on benefit income, living in rented accommodation in the subsidized local authority or housing association sector, many with more than one child. However, when we look in more detail, the picture is more complicated. Nearly half of the mothers were living with their own parents when the child was born. The majority (60 per cent) were in contact with the father at and after the birth. 38 per cent said that this was on at least a weekly basis. But 40 per cent were not in contact with him at that time. We will examine the quality of these relationships later (see p.69). Of course, the position did not remain static. How, then, did matters progress after the birth?

CHANGING FAMILY CIRCUMSTANCES

Household changes

Unlike longitudinal studies, which follow subjects over a period of time, our study was a cross-sectional one; our respondents were interviewed only once. However, the interviews took place at various points of time after the birth (Table 5.2), so our respondents could give us an account of what had occurred since the birth. All the children were still living with their mothers. Twenty-one (nearly half) had not moved house at all, but the rest (twenty-four out of forty-six) had. We know the ages of the children at the time of the first move in thirteen cases: in three the child was under 1, in eight it was between 1 and 2 and in two it was between 3 and 4.

There is some evidence therefore that moves tend to take place when the child is in its second year. Some of these were multiple moves. Three moved four times and two moved twice while the child was in its second year, and one moved four times in the first two years. There was a general move away from the mother's family into independent households. Twenty-one had been with the mother's parents when the child was born, but by the time of our interviews with them, only five mothers were still living with their own parents. Four of these were with young children (two were under one year and two were 2-year olds); the other child was 6. The move away from the maternal grandparental home therefore appears to take place mostly two or three years after the birth.

We do not know how far these moves would have weakened the relationship between the mother and child and the mother's parents, but we must not

Table 5.2: *Ages of Children at Interview—Never-together Group*

0–2	3–4	5–9	Over 10	Total
14	9	20	3	46

assume that leaving the grandparental home would necessarily have negative consequences. Research on the effects of joint upbringing by a mother and grandparents is inconclusive, but it is certainly possible that it is not necessarily more successful where the mother lives with the grandparents than where she lives independently from them.[9] Mothers who moved out of their parents' home would almost always find themselves in rented accommodation. One had moved into owner-occupation on marrying. The number of moves, however, poses risks to the maintenance of those relationships which constitute the child's social capital.[10]

Seven out of forty-six (15 per cent) of the children had acquired a stepfather by the time of the interview, three of whom had married the mother. If we add the three who had a stepfather at birth, we now have ten out of forty-six (22 per cent) of the children with a stepfather. Six were over 5 and four under 5. So only six of the 23 children (26 per cent) in the "never-together" group who were over 5 had a stepfather. Bradshaw and Millar (1991) estimated that lone-parenthood lasts four years on average. We cannot make a comparable estimate. However, it does appear from our data that, apart from an unknown number where the parents may later have partnered *with each other*, a majority of the households of this group of children were still one-parent households when the child reached the age of 5.

As we remarked earlier, in six cases the child later acquired a full sibling, but the father still did not join the household. In two cases the father was married to or living with another woman and it might appear that these men were creating "parallel families", which had no contact with each other. But by way of contrast, in another two cases the fathers were living at home with their parents, as was one of the mothers. It is not unrealistic to view this very small sub-group as possible instances of familial interaction between the wider families of both parents growing out of the joint parenthood of their son and daughter respectively. However, it turned out that in our cases the contact between the father and the children was not sustained.

Income and employment

The number of mothers in employment increased slightly after the birth of the children; four out of forty-two were now employed full-time and four out of forty-two part-time.[11] These proportions (9 per cent each) are slightly lower than the proportions of lone mothers who work according to the *General Household Survey* (13 per cent full-time, 16 per cent part-time) for 1994.[12] But our sample was not confined to "continuing" lone mothers; as we will see,

[9] McLanahan and Sandefur (1994: 30, 73–4).
[10] McLanahan and Sandefur (1994: 32).
[11] In this study we classify part-time work as employment for under sixteen hours a week.
[12] *General Household Survey 1994*, (OPCS, 1996), Table 7.9.

nine of the mothers later acquired a partner, and this may have influenced their propensity to seek employment. Those in full-time employment were women with higher educational qualifications, and were older than the rest (one 27, the others over 30), with older children. The part-timers were younger and had lower qualifications. Other mothers had had spells in employment, but only four had worked for any length of time. This reflects the low proportion of lone mothers in employment in the United Kingdom relative to other European countries. This is a difficult issue, raising wide issues (such as employment practices, availability of child-care facilities and the relationship between benefits, child support payments and earnings) which fall outside the present discussion.[13] It seemed clear that our unemployed mothers, living in subsidized housing without access to alternative income resources, could not afford to risk losing that subsidy by entering an uncertain labour market with low qualifications.

For the same reasons, household income levels remained low. Thirty-two out of forty-two (76 per cent) of the mothers depended primarily on state benefits at time of interview. This is a drop from forty-one out of forty-six (89 per cent) at the time of the children's birth, but still remains high. The rest depended on relatives (two), and on earned income (eight: five from their own employment, three from that of a partner). There were modest increases of income since the time of the birth of the children: the number whose household income was below £4,000 a year dropped from eighteen to fourteen; the number living on between £4,000 and £6,000 had increased from ten to fourteen; those with between £6,000 to £8,000 increased from six to nine and those with over £8,000 from one to six.[14]

Relationships between the parents

Except for the four male respondents, we had to rely on the mothers for information about the fathers and their relationships with them. We noted above (p. 63) the different groups into which they fell: the "already partnered fathers" (6/46); the "divorced/separated fathers" (6/46); the "at home fathers" (falling from seventeen to twelve by the time of interview); the "independent" fathers (15/46). We will use these categories in much of the analysis which follows.

Given the importance placed on the quality of *parental* relationships in some of the psychological studies on the well-being of children of disrupted families (see p. 55), the interviews incorporated a range of questions on these issues. Respondents were asked to evaluate the quality of their relationship

---

[13] See Bradshaw (1996).

[14] Note that in 1994, the income support entitlement for a mother with two children aged under 11 was £6,136 p.a.

with the other parent at about the time of the birth and at interview, being given the opportunity to describe it as good, bad or neither good nor bad. A number of respondents however preferred to answer that they had no relationship which could be recorded even in those terms. Table 5.3 examines the responses according to the category into which the father fell at the time of the child's birth.

Table 5.3: Relationship Between Parents at Birth and at Interview—Never-together Group

| State of relationship | Already partnered | Category of father at birth | | | | All |
		At home	Div/Sep	Indep	Unknown	
At birth						
Good	0	7	2	3	1	13
Neutral	2	1	0	2	0	5
Bad	0	4	1	3	0	8
No relationship	4	4	3	6	1	18
Unknown	0	1	0	1	0	2
Total	6	17	6	15	2	46
At interview						
Good	0	7	2	3	0	12
Neutral	0	2	1	3	0	6
Bad	0	1	0	1	0	2
No relationship	6	5	3	7	2	23
Unknown	0	2	0	1	0	3
Total	6	17	6	15	2	46

The best relationships, both at the time of the birth (seven out of seventeen: 41 per cent) and at interview, were found to be between mothers and fathers who were living with their parents at the time of the birth, though two out of six (one-third) of the parents who had divorced or separated before the birth had a good relationship then and maintained it. This contrasts quite strongly with the three out of fifteen (20 per cent) who enjoyed a good relationship with the fathers who were living independently. It is striking that *none* of the mothers reported a "good" relationship with the "already-partnered" fathers, though two had described the relationship as neither good nor bad when the chid was born. Indeed, these women were most likely to consider that they had no relationship at all with the father, and all saw it in this way at the time of the interview. Table 5.3 also shows that, if relationships did not generally improve over time, they generally became less bad for all groups of fathers. Closer analysis showed that the small number of "bad" relationships (five out of forty-six: 11 per cent) tended to fade into no relationship at all.

Decision-making

Much emphasis has been placed in discussions of cross-household parenting on how decisions concerning the children's care and upbringing are made. This, as we have seen (above pp. 37, 49–50) has been one area of uncertainty in the concept of parental responsibility. Recent research on men's roles has indicated stronger support for conventional roles than has recently been assumed to be the case.[15] We therefore asked about who took decisions concerning day-to-day care, taking the child to the doctor or dentist, buying clothes for the child, about holidays for the child and about matters concerning the child's school life. In all cases in this group except one the responsibility for these decisions was said to lie with the mothers. The exception was a case where the father bought clothes for his boys (an "at home" father), although he did not make any child support payments. In another case the mother noted that decision-making was shared with her new partner.

It must be conceded that these answers were given mainly (in forty-two out of forty-six cases) by the mothers. Maccoby and Mnookin (1992), in their study of parents with joint custody in California, found that the "outside" parents claimed to be more involved in decision-making than the parent who was looking after the child said they were. It may be that some of the fathers of our study children would have thought themselves more involved than the mothers saw them to be, though it is notable that the four male respondents (who were "outside" fathers) did not dissent from the general view. There is, however, certainly no evidence of any degree of decision-making involvement of the fathers in any of our categories who had never shared a household with the mother and the child.

CONTACT BETWEEN FATHERS AND THE STUDY CHILD

Contact can be measured in crude terms involving the total period of time a parent is "with" the child. However, in replacing the term "access" by the broader word "contact", the Children Act 1989 sought to include within the regulatory framework other forms of communication, such as letter-writing. We wished to interpret "contact" within this wider spirit, as indicative of a serious commitment by a parent to the child. As we looked at our data it became clear that there were many forms in which this commitment could be expressed. While in a standard case this might take the form of weekly visits for children under 5, and visits every fortnight with an overnight stay for older

---

[15] Dench (1996).

children, we were loath to exclude cases where, say, a parent who lives abroad has the children to visit for a few weeks every year during the summer holidays.

For our analysis, then, we have divided the families into three groups, all roughly equal. The first group of "in-contact" fathers comprised sixteen out of forty-six (35 per cent) cases where we judged that the father was showing the kind of commitment we have referred to, with visits at least once a month or where overnight stays are a regular feature. We classified eighteen out of forty-six (39 per cent) of cases as being where the father was "out-of-contact" (though in three very minimal contact had occurred: in one there had been one telephone call, and nothing else; in the other the child was invited for a holiday abroad, but did not go and nothing else happened and in a third contact had occurred only three times in seven years). Nor did we consider that making contribution in cash or kind in itself amounted to contact. Then there were six cases where contact had started for a few weeks immediately after the child was born but failed to take hold (the "false starts") and another six where it had taken root but later stopped: the "interrupted contact" group. In effect, in these last twelve cases, contact was lost.

The broad picture is that, in this section of our sample where the child never shared a household with its father, in one third of cases an apparently continuing relationship was established between the child and the father. This can last a long time. Of the 23 children in this "never-together" group who were over 5 at time of interview, six (slightly over a quarter) had retained such contact. However, for six other children in the group, contact seemed to be established at first, but later stopped. So in twenty-two out of forty-six (nearly half) of the cases regular contact began from the time of the birth, although in six cases it had not survived to the time of interview. There was therefore no general tendency in these men to "walk away" immediately after the birth, as is sometimes held, even though they had never lived with the child. But we needed to look more closely and see what kinds of factors might be associated with the continuing exercise or non-exercise of contact.

Category of father at child's birth

The first factor to consider is the category into which the father fell when the child was born (Table 5.4).

As might be expected from the information about parental relationships, the strongest association is with the father living at his parents' home when the child was born: nine out of seventeen (53 per cent) of these fathers were still in contact with the children at the time of interview compared to five out of fifteen (33 per cent) of the fathers who had been living independently. Of the "at home" fathers still in contact, however, a very important qualification must be made. In all those cases, the children were very young; seven were

Table 5.4: Contact and Category of Father at Child's Birth—Never-together Group

Category of father	Type of contact Continuing contact	No contact	False starts	Interrupted contact	All
Already partnered	0	5	0	1	6
Independent	5	7	2	1	15
At home	9	4	3	1	17
Div/Sep from mother	2	2	1	1	6
Unknown	0	0	0	2	2
Totals	16	18	6	6	46

under 3, and the other two were aged 4 and 5. While only five "independent" fathers were in contact, the youngest of these children was 4, the others being 5, 7, 8 and 11. So while the fact that the father is living with his parents at the time of the birth is strongly associated with his continuing contact with the child, this might not last. We might speculate however whether the exercise of contact by these men might be a consequence of the involvement of their own parents in the situation and perhaps even the establishment by them of a grandparental relationship with the child, which could provide, at the very least, a suitable venue for receiving visits from the child. It is also important to note that fathers who were living with their own parents had not repartnered (the issue of repartnering is discussed below, pp. 76–7). By the time of interview seven out of twelve (58 per cent) of the fathers *still* living at home retained contact while five out of twelve (42 per cent) had lost it.

Five of the six "already partnered" fathers were completely out of contact with the child; the sixth made contact only after his existing partnership broke down, but abandoned it when he formed a new relationship. These men were effectively unavailable to the study children. Of course, had their fathers broken with their wives/cohabitants (and children) and joined the study child's household, that would have removed the case from the present sample, although it might have entered our study with respect to the father's first group of children. Policy discussion has focused very much on family relationships, and obligations, when men father children and subsequently go on to establish "second" families. The obligation to the "external" child is somehow seen as "prior" to that towards his later family. But here the sequence is reversed. A man with an established family fathers a child outside it. Our data suggests that in such circumstances people do not *act* as if the obligation to the outside child were very strong.

Two parents in the "divorced/separated" group maintained contact, but the other four did not manage this successfully. So it appears that children whose mothers had previously been married to or lived with the father were no more likely to keep in contact with their father than were the rest of the children in this group.[16]

Distance from child

It might be thought that the distance at which the father lives from the child would have some bearing on the continuation of contact, and it clearly does (Table 5.5).

Table 5.5: *Distance at which Father Lives from Child—Never-together Group*

| | Type of contact | | | | |
	Continuing contact	No contact	False starts	Interrupted contact	All
Distance from child					
Under 10 miles	13	8	5	3	29
Over 10 miles	3	9	1	2	15
Unknown	0	1	0	1	2
Totals	16	18	6	6	46

Of those in contact, most (thirteen out of sixteen) lived within ten miles of the child. However, living close to the child did not necessarily predispose towards contact. Sixteen out of twenty-nine (55 per cent) of cases where there was either no contact or where it failed to take root, or later terminated, involved fathers who were living within ten miles. Furthermore, moving away from the vicinity may just as well be a result of lack of contact as a cause of it. However, two men lived some 50 miles away and one over 300 miles away, and yet maintained weekly contact. They had kept contact regularly from the child's birth, although one had to adjust from daily contact with his one-year-old son to Sundays only during a period of shift work, and another had been unable to see his children during a spell in prison, but resumed overnight contacts after his release.

Contact, employment and financial support

It was difficult to know whether there was any relationship between the fathers' employment status and the exercise of contact because the lack of contact restricted the information reported to us on this issue (Table 5.6 (a)).

[16] It must be remembered that in these cases parents separated *before* the child was born. The position is different where married people separate after the child's birth (see Ch 7).

Table 5.6: Contact, Employment and Financial Support—Never-together Group

(a) Contact and Employment

Work status of father	Type of contact				
	Continuing contact	No contact	False starts	Interrupted contact	All
Full-time	10	7	3	3	23
Unemployed	4	3	2	2	11
Part-time and other	2	0	0	1	3
Unknown	0	8	1	0	9
Totals	16	18	6	6	46

(b) Contact and financial support

Support paid	Type of contact				
	Continuing contact	No contact	False starts	Interrupted contact	All
Yes	9*	1	0	2	12
Irregular	4	0	0	0	4
No	2	17	6	3	28
Unknown	1	0	0	1	2
Totals	16	18	6	6	46

(c) Child Support Agency approach to father

CSA approach	Type of contact				
	Continuing contact	No contact	False starts	Interrupted contact	All
Yes	11	8	2	5	26
No	0	0	0	0	0
Unknown	5	10	4	1	20
Totals	16	18	6	6	46

*Two "in kind" only.

Whether there is any relationship between employment status and exercise of contact remains tantalisingly unclear. There is, however, a link between the provision of financial support and the exercise of contact, as Table 5.6(b) demonstrates. Generally, financial support was infrequent. Regular payments occurred in only in twelve out of forty-six (26 per cent) of cases. The fathers who were out of contact paid little or nothing. However, those who were in contact were usually paying something (nine out of sixteen: 56 per cent), though two were contributing "in kind" only. The Child Support Agency was in its second year when the interviews were conducted and it will be seen that the Agency was known to have contacted many of the fathers (Table 5.6(c)), although many of them were in contact and paying already. In the other cases where Agency contact was reported, the respondents seldom believed the father was paying anything. The fathers who were giving some financial support were paying small, regular, weekly sums. One paid £2, in accordance with Child Support Agency Assessment, following a period of unemployment, and another a nominal 5 pence. The other payments seemed to be under voluntary agreements; two paid £10, three paid £20 and one paid £30. These sums were rather lower than would be expected under Child Support Agency Assessment, the average of which were about £23 a week at that time (they have fallen slightly since 1995).[17] Although respondents were explicitly asked whether there was a court order, we were not confident about how they interpreted "court order". In only one case was a father said to be paying the amount he had been ordered to pay by a court (£30 a week for three children) and it was said that he was not complying in two other cases, although in one he was unemployed.

While we see a relationship between ongoing contact and the payment of support, at least where the fathers are able to pay it, there were a few fathers who were in contact but not paying financial support. It did not seem that the fathers were exercising contact *because* they were giving material assistance. Rather, the slight excess of contact over support suggests that exercising contact creates a disposition to support. Perhaps therefore we should not be concerned that enforcement of the support obligation will automatically lead to more attempts to enforce contact. Furthermore, there was no evidence that the interventions of the Agency had disrupted the exercise of contact.

Among the reasons why the father was not paying financial support could be that he was unemployed or that he had subsequently partnered and gave absolute priority to his second family. Unfortunately, we lacked information about employment status or the occurrence of partnering by the father in ten cases. Of the remaining nineteen, nine (47 per cent) were unemployed and ten (53 per cent) had a partner (some fell in both categories). In fact we found only one case where the father was living with another woman where he had paid support, and in that case the new relationship had broken down. That leaves four out of nineteen (21 per cent) who were working full time and did not, apparently, have a partner and still did not pay anything. There could therefore have been some resources here which should have been available to the study children and on which no other partner or child had a claim. We are reminded of the findings in our previous study (Eekelaar and Maclean (1986)) that, while such (untapped) resources appeared clearly to exist, they did not seem to be on a large scale; in the present sample, they appeared in only seven out of forty-six (15 per cent) of all cases in the "never-together" group. Of course it is arguable that those with a new partner could or should

[17] Child Support Agency, *Quarterly Summary of Statistics* (August 1996).

have paid something, as the Child Support Act 1991 requires (see pp. 38–9). We will return to this issue later (pp. 149–52).

Contact and subsequent partnering

We have mentioned that fathers who now had a partner (or who stayed with the partner with whom they were living when the child was born) did not pay any support to the child. Did they have any contact with the child either? The results are shown in Table 5.7.

Table 5.7: Contact and Partnering—Never-together Group

	(a) Contact and subsequent partnering				
Parents'		Type of contact			
partnering	Continuing contact	No contact	False starts	Interrupted	All
Father only subs. p'tner	1	2	1	4	8
Mother only subs. p'tner	0	4	1	0	5
Both subs. p'tner	1	3	0	0	4
Neither subs. partner	14	6	4	2	26
Unknown	0	3	0	0	3
Totals	16	18	6	6	46

	(b) Contact by whether either parent in pre-existing or new partnership				
		Type of contact			
	Continuing contact	No contact	False starts	Interrupted	All
In p'ship	2	12	2	4	20
Not in p'ship	14	6	4	2	26
Totals	16	18	6	6	46

Table 5.7(a) shows that when there is no contact between the child and the father, nine out of eighteen (50 per cent) of the parents had acquired a partner by the time of the interview (mothers slightly more often than fathers). We do not know whether this was relevant to the failure of the father to establish contact. It might not be relevant since he had not been in contact

before she formed the partnership. On the other hand, it might be relevant if the mother had been contemplating the partnership from around the time of the child's birth. In fact, none of the mothers in the "no-contact" cases were living with another man at the time of the child's birth. However, existing contact tended to be *interrupted* (and effectively lost) more by the acquisition of a partner by the father than by the mother, though in one case the mother's partnering appeared to prevent contact from taking root and in another the mother was already partnered to another man when the child was born.

The Table also shows that more fathers acquired partners than mothers (twelve fathers, nine mothers), and this was especially so in the "interrupted contact" group, where no mother, but four fathers, had acquired a later partner, suggesting that the fathers' acquisition of partners could have been a significant factor in the loss of contact. It does not, however, appear to have been significant where contact failed to take root (the "false starts"), where one mother and one father acquired a later partner. These cases are discussed further below (p. 80).

Table 5.7(a) does not, however, give the full picture regarding the effect of partnerships on contact because it includes the case where an already partnered father "changed partners" after the child's birth and excludes those cases where a parent was partnered to someone other than the other parent at the time of the child's birth and that partnership was still subsisting at interview. Table 5.7(b) therefore shows the occasions when either parent was living in a partnership at the time of interview, irrespective of whether the partnership began before or after the child's birth. The association between the existence of such partnerships and the lack of, or disruption of, contact is very striking: in fourteen of the sixteen cases where contact was continuing neither parent was in a partnership.

Such partnering is of course often accompanied by the birth of new children, and this was usually the case. But sometimes a parent might have new children without acquiring a new partner. As we have said, we could not know to what extent this occurred among the fathers. We know that two of the "in-contact" mothers had later children by other fathers without repartnering. Curiously, the two cases in the "never-together" group where the mothers had later children by the same father as that of the study child were not those in which contact was continued.

CONCLUSIONS

We introduce our discussion of the data with a closer description of three specific cases. We have stressed that this group of children have experienced such differing familial experiences that generalizing about the group as a whole is unhelpful. On the other hand, analysis must go beyond the mere cataloguing of individual instances. It is necessary to see if there is some deeper structure, if not of cause and effect, then at least of association between various factors. This might allow some sets of circumstances to be seen as providing "typologies", standard cases subject, however, to many variations of detail. We choose three cases as illustrating three such typologies (the names of course are fictitious).

Robert

The story of Robert, 5 when the interview took place, and his family is relatively straightforward. He was born to Emma. Emma was then 23 and was living in a house rented from a housing association, on her own but with a one-year-old baby son of a man she no longer saw. Robert's father, Noel, was unemployed, and still living at home with his parents. Emma and Noel were on good terms, and were in touch with each other every day at the time Robert was born. The following year Emma had another little boy, but she was reluctant to confirm that Noel was the father. She had now moved to another housing association house, and was still receiving Income Support, as she had been doing continuously since Robert's birth. The good relationship with Noel was still continuing. He lived less than ten miles away, and saw Robert three or four times a week, but never stayed with him overnight. Noel did not, however, share in significant decisions about Robert's upbringing, except for the purchase of clothes. When Robert was born, there had been no arrangement about financial support and Noel never provided any, except for birthday presents and buying clothes for Robert at Christmas. No contact has been made with the Child Support Agency. The birth of the third child had not affected Robert's relationship with his father in any way.

In this case, then, a pattern of parenting had been established immediately upon the child's birth and had been sustained throughout the first year. The birth of another child, possibly by another man, had not disrupted this relationship, which could continue because the father lived close by. The law never became involved, and the lack of resources of both parents meant that any financial re-ordering would be pointless. Although Robert is now only 5, short of either of the parents moving, it seems likely that this pattern will continue. However, were either of his parents, especially Noel, to form a partnership with someone, the continuation of the relationship between Robert and his father will be at serious risk. If Noel acquires a job, it seems that Emma will expect some support from him, for she thought that men should support their own children in priority to their new partner. Even if she were to acquire a husband later, she would think that Noel should continue to pay something.

Jane

Compare Robert's story with that of Jane, who was 8 years old at the time of the interview. We know of her only through the account by her father, Fred. Fred was a married man, a father of three, when, out of work, he had an affair with Christine, who was also out of work and living with her parents. When Jane was born, Fred and Christine agreed that he would have no contact with her, and make no contribution to her support. Nor did he continue to have any communications with Christine. Fred had been in and out of work since Jane was born, but made no attempt to see her, even though he lived within ten miles of her. However, the Child Support Agency had made contact with him. Fred hoped, however, that Christine might have a new partner who would be willing to adopt Jane, thus (he thought, correctly) absolving him from support liability. For although Fred believed that if a child's parents split up when neither is at fault the father should support the child, he did not think a father should continue to pay if the mother re-married.

Carol

George also believed that the father's obligation should cease when the mother re-marries. He was 23 at time of interview, and was in full-time work four years earlier when his child, Carol, was born. Carol's mother, Karen, was then living in a council flat on her own, while George was living at home with his parents, brothers and sisters. Indeed, he was still living there at the time of the interview. Initially George saw Carol twice a week by informal agreement with Karen. But when Carol was 4 months old, another man, Stephen, moved in with Karen. That had two consequences for George. First, probably at Stephen's instigation, Karen began to find obstacles to the visits, and these gradually faded out. George had seen Carol only once in the last three years. Secondly, Karen obtained a court order against George for child support of £20 a week. But this was never paid. However, a year later the sum was reduced to £14, and this has since been paid regularly. But a few months ago Stephen and Karen (who had married one another), separated.

Looked at from Carol's point of view, Stephen's arrival seems to have been most unfortunate. It brought about the termination, perhaps permanently, of the visits of her father, who wanted to keep them up, and who was in a good position to support her, and introduce her to his wider kin network. She does not, however, seem to have acquired a new "father" in return, for Stephen has now left. Worse, Stephen is seen by George as having taken over his responsibilities to support Carol, and indeed he obtained a reduction in his support obligation for that reason. Carol's birth occurred before the Child Support Act 1991 became effective, so it is unlikely that such a reduction would occur under the new system. Nevertheless, George's belief that the new adult male in the family takes over the financial responsibilities for the child will not assist any sense of obligation he might have towards Carol. Whether this might revive now that Stephen has left is unknown, though we may surmise that the chances of it doing so after such a complete severance of the relationship is unlikely. So perhaps here the parties, or at least the child, were not well served by being left, initially at any rate, largely to themselves, with only a residual, and largely ineffectual, court order.

These three cases and the data reveal the fluidity which family relationships can have in the "never-together" group. One in five of the children in our whole sample do not even *start* their lives in the conventional "two birth-parent" household. But the degrees of "deviance" from that model are highly variable. "Serious" contact with fathers who had never lived in the same household as the child began in almost half of these cases, but, by the time of interview, it had ceased in about one-quarter of them. Nevertheless, another quarter of the children experienced at least five years of contact with the father of a kind which showed commitment on his part to having a relationship with the child, and, as in the case of Robert (p. 78) this was continuing at the time of the interview. For the younger children contact was also continuing, but mostly when the father was living at his own parents' home. However, in all but one case the main decisions about the child's upbringing rested with the mother.

It was not easy to discern why in some cases contact started but failed to become established: the "false starts". Six fathers saw the child only during its first year of life, four of them for only the first few weeks. Contact had been made but never seriously took root. It might be thought that these "false start" fathers would share characteristics with the out-of-contact fathers: to live far away, and to have other familial commitments. But that was not so (Tables 5.5, 5.7(a)). Five of the seven fathers were still without a partner, and four of them lived close by. Three were still living with their parents. This was a very similar proportion to those who established continuing contact. However, the relationships between the parents were worse, two-thirds reporting it as being bad.

In two of the five cases where the father had not found a partner the relationship seemed to end because of the mother's wishes. In one she felt the visits were unreliable and caused the child distress; in the other she had acquired a partner and the father felt unwanted when the stepfather "became Dad". In the other three (two of them involving fathers who were students), after an initial visit or two, the child simply did not seem to become part of the fathers' young, fast-changing, lives. It seems therefore that there are some cases even where the father is in close proximity to the child and has no other familial commitments and where he could offer social capital to the child where his disposition, or life-style, or the mother's wishes, prevents him establishing any relationship with the child. But these seem to be a small proportion of cases. However, it might be added that these men did not always escape possible financial responsibility. There were three court orders which were not complied with and two men had been contacted by the Child Support Agency.

In five cases contact had ended entirely. In three of these cases this was at the request of the mother who felt that contact was bad for the child; the fathers were described as being "irresponsible". In another case the father had moved in with an aunt (!) who had been involved in accusations of child abuse and in another he went abroad after irregular contact with a child who was now 15. It is notable how many cases in this small sub-group involved later partnering. Four out of six of the fathers acquired a later partner, and one mother retained her earlier partner. (One father went abroad). While the mother might instigate the break on the ground of the father's "unreliability" or "irresponsibility", this may have been linked to a perception of his behaviour involving his new girlfriend. While we have conceded that the causal connection between the later acquisition of a partner, by either parent, and the continuation of contact is a complex matter, it remains that only two out of sixteen (12 per cent) of the in-contact fathers had subsequently partnered compared to five out of twelve (42 per cent) in the "false starts and interrupted" group. And of course nearly half those who never made any contact at all were in existing relationships from the beginning. Similarly, only one mother in the in-contact group acquired a partner later, compared to seven out of eighteen (39 per cent) of those where contact was never established and one of the "false starts and interrupted" group.

The last case of this second sub-group was unusual insofar as the mother had approached a solicitor to seek a court order to *require* the father, who had hitherto taken little interest in two boys, aged one and 4, to accept them for overnight visits. There were no new partners involved, nor had any support been paid.

It seemed as if a very important factor in allowing the parental role to develop was the absence of a partner for either parent. It is even possible that the parents were delaying acquiring a partner in order to safeguard the relationship. A father who was living at home was more likely to have retained a relationship with the child and less likely to have acquired a partner. Such partnering did not always spell the end of the relationship between the father and child (sometimes it helped it), but mostly it does seem to have made it very difficult. It seems that this can usually only be counted as a loss for the child. If the mother acquires a partner, the loss might be offset by the acquisition of a stepfather, and its accompanying material advantages, but we saw in Carol's case (p. 79) that this could be short-lived. If the father already has a family, he is unlikely to play a part in the child's life. The only way in which the father could establish a secure "conventional" family household with the study child would be to withdraw from the first child. As Jane's case shows (p. 78), her potential relationship with her father is sacrificed for the security of his existing family.

These cases are also notable for the relative lack of involvement of third parties in brokering contact arrangements between the parents. Solicitors were consulted in only two cases (one being where the mother wanted the father to play a larger role, the other being where the mother sought advice as to how to arrange visits). Even over the question of money, the Child Support Agency had become involved in twenty-five out of forty-six cases in all, which is perhaps surprisingly low given the high proportion of mothers who were on benefit both when the children were born and afterwards. These mothers, and their children, are generally poor. They rely heavily on state benefits. Yet they suffer relatively little long-term conflict with the fathers, and in some cases enjoy a good relationship with him. But the fathers are generally not in a position to help them very much financially and there is always the risk that they might find a partner and withdraw. If the mother finds a partner she will probably be better off financially, but the relationship between the child and the father may also suffer. The pull of familial relationships within the household is very strong in these cases. We might liken those relationships which develop between the fathers and children in this group to fragile threads, occurring more frequently than might have been thought and capable of being nurtured, but which frequently lack a source of strength to enable them to survive challenges posed by changes in household structure. What the source of such strength may be we will consider in later chapters.

6

Children Whose Parents Cohabited Outside Marriage

We now move to those children whose parents were living together when the child was born, but who were not married to each other at that time. Although researchers are now paying more attention to cohabitation outside marriage, there is still relatively little information about how adults who live in such unions compare *as parents* to other groups of parents. The "marriage saving" concerns which accompanied the enactment of the divorce scheme contained in the Family Law Act 1996 took into account only the effects of parental separation on the children of married parents. On the other hand, the Child Support Act 1991 swept all absent parents, whether previously married or not, within its scope. This chapter identifies the children of parents who had lived together with the child, but without marrying each other, as a distinct group and initiates a process of comparison between this group and the other categories of children in the study.

As this study is constructed around the children rather than the parents we needed to find a term to describe this group. The "former cohabiting parent" group seemed to capture their situation best. There were fifty-one such children, constituting 20 per cent of our sample, which, as we have noted, is almost identical to the percentage of children born to apparently unmarried cohabiting couples in 1994 (p. 60). Of course, our fifty-one children are not a sub-set of that segment of the child population because to qualify for our sample the parents had to have separated and remained apart. We compare our sample with *General Household Survey* data below (pp. 106–7). Of our fifty-one respondents, forty-three were mothers and eight were fathers. As for the previous group we did not receive the same quantity of information from mothers and fathers and we have indicated where the information came from only one group and when it was combined.

Mike Murphy (1995) has underlined the difficulty of reliably comparing breakdown "rates" of unmarried cohabitants and married people (see p. 21). Although information about the stability of unmarried cohabitation is welcome, it is difficult to know what conclusions to draw from comparing their stability with that of marriages. After all, unmarried cohabitants may vary very widely with regard to their own intentions as to the nature of their relationship, whereas people who marry at least outwardly profess a public commitment to making a serious attempt at long-term partnership. However it is useful to be able to compare the stability of the cohabitation of unmarried *parents* with that of married parents because each couple has commenced the joint enterprise of bearing and bringing up a child and the separation of parents has consequences for their children. It may therefore be helpful to know that, in our cross-sectional sample, if we exclude those who had never lived together, one-quarter of the parents were former unmarried cohabitants and the rest were formerly married parents. Given that the parents of 21 per cent of children born in 1994 to parents who were living together were not married to each other (see p. 20), our sample suggests that the "breakdown" rate between the unmarried cohabiting parents may be rather higher than that for married parents, especially as our sample was taken from a population which had formed families many years earlier than 1994 when even fewer people cohabited (and had children) without marrying. It also seems that these relationships break down rather quicker than marriages, as will be seen later (p. 123).

CHARACTERISTICS OF THIS GROUP

The group comprised fifty-one respondents (forty-three women and eight men). In the "never-together" group, all the study children were living with the mother. In the present group, three of the study children were living with the father. In one case the child's sibling was living with the mother in an arrangement where the children were "split" between the households. There were two other cases where siblings were split; in these the fathers were looking after siblings of study children who were living with the mother. At time of interview, the mothers, and therefore also the children, were older than those in the "never-together" group; not surprisingly, since they had experienced a period of cohabitation with the father before the separation, which most of the "never-togethers" had not. Indeed, seven parents (six mothers and one father) had been married to someone else before starting to live with the study child's father. These "post-marital" cohabitants therefore comprised 14 per cent of this group. Kiernan and Estaugh (1993: 11) report that in 1989 34 per cent of cohabitants had been previously married. But that includes all cohabitants, including "post-marital" cohabitants who might have no children or who were living with a child or children of only one of them, whereas our sample was restricted to former cohabitants who were both parents of the study child, and are therefore a sub-group within all post-marital cohabitants.

In case the presence of even a small number of post-marital cohabitants, who could have distinctive features of their own, might weaken some of the comparisons we wish to make, we sometimes either excluded them from certain comparisons or recorded their data separately. For example, they were slightly older than the other former cohabitants, who themselves were older than the parents in the "never-together" group. The former cohabiting mothers were also older than those in the "never-together" group when the study child had been born, suggesting that if parents are to have a child when living together, the onset of parenthood will be delayed, either because they need time to find a place in which to live, or have deliberately postponed the birth while they have cohabited (or both) (Table 6.1). The children in the "never-together" group may well have been unplanned.

When we describe the events that took place since the separation, it is important to know the length of time which had elapsed since that occurred.

Table 6.1: Ages of Mothers and Children—Never-together and Former Cohabiting Parent Groups*

(a) Age of mothers at time of interview

Age	Never-together group n = 42 %	Cohabiting parent group	
		never-married n = 37 %	post-marital n = 6 %
Under 30	68	47	40
30–39	27	42	20
Over 40	5	11	40

(b) Age of children living with mothers at time of interview

Age	Never-together group n = 42 %	Cohabiting parent group	
		never-married n = 37 %	post-marital n = 6 %
Under 2	24	7	17
2–4	26	22	0
5–6	24	16	0
7–10	20	30	50
Over 10	6	22	33

(c) Age of mother at birth of study child

Age	Never-together group n = 42 %	Cohabiting parent group	
		never-married n = 37 %	post-marital n = 6 %
Under 20	32	16	20
20–24	39	24	20
25–29	14	42	20
30–35	7	11	40
Over 35	5	8	0

* To enable comparisons to be made between the groups, we have used percentages, although the numbers in some some-groups are small.

For the "never-together" group there had been no cohabitation and thus no separation after the child's birth, so for comparison in their case we treat the time of the child's birth as a notional separation. The two groups have similar profiles in this regard (Table 6.2). Three-quarters of the interviews in both groups took place within seven years of the birth or separation, though more were conducted after ten years in the case of the former cohabiting parents than of the 'never-together' group. Nevertheless, in comparing the groups as regards events subsequent to the birth or separation, we are dealing with very similar time-periods.

Table 6.2: Time Between Birth/Separation and Interview—Never-together and Former Cohabiting Parent Groups

Group	Number of years since separation/birth				
	Under 2 %	2–4 %	5–6 %	7–10 %	Over 10 %
Former cohabiting group (n = 51)	25	31	20	6	18
Never-together group (n = 46)	24	26	24	20	6

CHARACTERISTICS OF FAMILY OF ORIGIN OF THE CHILDREN

The major difference between the children in the present group and the "never-togethers" is of course the presence of the father in the household when they were born. We wanted to discover how significant this factor was in contributing to the child's social capital. It seems that the presence of the father is associated with a higher proportion living in the owner-occupied sector than was the case for the "never-togethers". Excluding the seven post-marital cohabitants,[1] twelve out of forty-four (27 per cent) were in owner-occupation immediately before separation compared to 10 per cent of the "never-together" group (or 5 per cent if we exclude from that group those who had lived together *before* the child was born). This is very much lower than the position for all families with dependent children, of which 76 per cent were in owner-occupation in 1993/4.[2] Reliance on state benefits was high in both groups. Benefits were reported as having been the main source of income before separation in fifteen out of forty-four (34 per cent) cases. This compares to 93 per cent of the mothers in the "never-together" group who reported similarly for the period around the child's birth (see p. 65).

This suggests that many of the men were unemployed during the cohabitation, and so it was. Again, excluding the post-marital cohabitants, only twenty-four out of forty-four (55 per cent) of the partners of the mothers were

[1] Only one post-marital cohabitant family was living in owner-occupation.
[2] *General Household Survey 1994* (OPCS, 1996), Table 2.16.

in full-time employment at the time of the separation; seventeen out of forty-four (39 per cent) were not in work (we lacked information about three men). The information on the fathers in the "never-together" group was insufficient in this respect to make a comparison. As for the mothers, only three out of forty-one (7 per cent) in the "never-together" group had been in full-time employment when the child was born, and none part-time, though the numbers employed increased as time went on (to 9 per cent full-time and 9 per cent part-time). But in the present group, seven out of forty-four (16 per cent) had been in full-time employment and another ten out of forty-four (23 per cent) had been working part-time at the time of the separation, so that 39 per cent were employed and 61 per cent were not (Table 6.3). Perhaps the higher level of part-time working among the former cohabitants than the "never-togethers" is accounted for by the greater ease of arranging part-time employment when a partner (particularly one who is unemployed) is available to help with child care.

Table 6.3: Main Source of Income and Employment Immediately Before Birth/ Separation—Never-together and Former Cohabiting Parent Groups

Main income source	Never-together group n = 46 %	Former cohabiting parent group n = 44* %
Social Sec. benefit	89	34
Father in FT employment	—[+]	57
Mother in FT employment	7	16
Mother in PT employment	0	23

* Excludes post-marital cohabitants
[+] Insufficient information

The employment rate of the men fell well below the national rate for men between 25 and 49 (84 per cent in 1994) and that of the women differed from the employment rate for married women with dependent children (22 per cent full-time; 42 per cent part-time) largely in the lower proportion working part-time.[3] It would seem that cohabiting men, or, more precisely and perhaps significantly, men in cohabitations which subsequently break down, are much less likely to be in secure employment than those in the population at large (for married men, see p. 109), while the employment pattern of the women falls between that of married women with children and of lone mothers generally (13 per cent of whom worked full-time and 16 per cent part-time in 1992–94[4]).

[3] The employment statistics are taken from General Household Survey 1994, Tables 7.3(a) and 7.9. Definitions of employment can be controversial, and our comparisons on this can reflect orders of magnitude only.
[4] General Household Survey 1994, Table 7.9.

Table 6.4: Educational Qualifications of Mothers—Never-together and Former Cohabiting Parent Groups

Qualification	Never-together group n = 42 %	Former cohabiting parent group	
		never-married n = 37 %	post-marital n = 6 %
No qualification	40	32	34
GCE or GCSE	47	37	66
A levels	2	8	0
Vocational	2	10	0
Degree or diploma	9	13	0

The former cohabitants had higher educational qualifications than the mothers in the "never-together" group, but this was not very marked except for the small number of post-marital cohabitants (Table 6.4).

The gross household income of the former cohabiting parents was higher than for the "never-together" group. Of the mothers of the "never-together" group who were living independently of their parents (n = 23), 87 per cent received under £6,000 and the rest received a little over £6,000. Of all the former cohabiting parents about whom we had the information (n = 48), 39 per cent received under £6,000 (21 per cent under £4,000). Six per cent reported incomes of about £18,000 (Table 6.5) whereas none in the "never-together" group received as much as that. But the general level of incomes of the former cohabiting parents was considerably lower than those reported for cohabiting parents with children by Kiernan and Estaugh for 1989 (1993: 17), where only 40 per cent had weekly incomes below £200 (about £10,000 a year), compared to our 67 per cent. Similarly, Kiernan and Estaugh found more in owner-occupation (39 per cent compared to our 27 per cent) and fewer partners to be unemployed (19 per cent compared to our 39 per cent). But our sample is of course of *former* cohabiting parents; those whose cohabitations broke down. Their apparently lower economic profile compared to that of cohabitants in general can be taken as evidence that the widely known association between *marital* breakdown and economic adversity, particularly unemployment,[5] applies also to unmarried cohabitation.

CHANGES IN FAMILY CIRCUMSTANCES

Financial effects

The most significant change for this group was the departure of a parent. In forty-six out of fifty-one (90 per cent) of cases the children had stayed with

[5] See Gibson (1996: 13–14).

Table 6.5: Incomes of Former Cohabiting Parents Before Separation n = 48*

Income	Cumulative %
Under £6,000	39
£6,001 to £10,000	67
£10,001 to £16,000	94
Over £16,000	100

*Information unavailable in 3 cases

the mother, though, as we will describe, in two of these the children subsequently left the maternal home. Table 6.6 charts the employment and financial circumstances of the mothers as they changed over time.

It will be seen that immediately after the separation the percentage of families relying on state benefits as the main source of income rose from 37 to 75 per cent and the gross household incomes dropped sharply from an already low base. However, they had recovered to some extent by the time of interview to a position similar to that before the separation. Even so, two-thirds had incomes below £8,000, and relied on social security as their main source. The loss of the fathers' earnings had been replaced partly by an increase in the proportions of mothers who relied on their own earnings (from 9 to 18 per cent) and the earnings of a new partner. But this did not mean that more women went out to work. On the contrary, fewer did. This was especially marked for the part-time workers. They tended now to depend either on social security (perhaps because they could no longer rely upon their partner for help with child care) or on their new partner's earnings. In fact, new partners played only a moderate role in improving the financial position of these women. Of the eight women who repartnered, five were still on social security; only three reported the new partner's income as the main source at time of interview (although in one case it brought about a very considerable improvement from her financial situation during the cohabitation). It seems that new partners made less of an improvement to the household income than one might expect. 57 per cent of the mothers who had not repartnered were not working at the time of interview. One mother said she was relying substantially on her former partner, which is interesting as there is no legal obligation on the former partner to support her except to the extent that it is covered by the duty to pay child support.

Housing changes

Thirteen of the study children were living in owner-occupied homes at the time of their parents' separation and eight (64 per cent) stayed after the

Table 6.6: Employment and Income Changes over Time—Former Cohabiting Parent Group

(a) Employment of mothers

Employment	Before separation	At interview	
		All mothers	Non-repartnered mother
	n = 51	n = 51	n = 40
	%	%	%
Full-time	16	16	20
Part-time	20	9	10
Unemployed	57	61	57
Full-time ed.	2	4	5
Sick	2	2	2
Unclear	2	6	5

(b) Main source of income of mothers[+]

Main income source	Before separation n = 51 %	After separation n = 43[+] %	At interview n = 43[+] %
Social security b'ft	37	75	66
Mother's earnings	9	16	18
Father's earnings	37	–	–
Father's earnings plus social security	4	–	–
Both mother's and father's earnings	4	–	–
Maintenance	–	2	4
New p'tner's earnings	–	–	7
New p'tner's and mother's earnings	–	–	2
Relatives	2	2	0
Unclear	6	0	0

(c) Income levels of mothers[+]

Income	Before separation n = 46[*] Cum %	After separation n = 40[**] Cum %	At interview n = 41[***] Cum %
Under £4,000	19	55	15
£4,001 to £6,000	39	80	51
£6,001 to £8,000	56	85	68
£8,001 to £10,000	67	90	76
£10,001 to £12,000	74	90	80
£12,001 to £15,000	91	97	93
Over £15,000	100	100	100

[+] Mothers only reporting
[*] Information missing in 5 cases
[**] Information from women only; incomplete in 2 cases
[***] Information from women only; incomplete in 1 case

separation, at least for some time. But the circumstances varied greatly. The house was in the mother's name in two cases, and in a grandparent's name in one. So in three of the eight cases the mother continued to live in a house belonging to herself or her family. Of the remaining five cases, one house was in the father's name and was given to the mother in what the mother, in language usually used for divorcing couples, described as a "clean break", though no court order was involved. She later sold the house. In another it was in the father's name, but he still continued to "come and go". In three cases the house had been in joint names and the mother continued to live in it (though one mother later burnt it down). In four cases the child moved and the father stayed; two involved a house belonging to the father and one a house belonging to his parents. In the third case where the child moved the mother sold the house which was hers and in the fourth the father stayed with another child in a split custody arrangement. In the final case they all moved and the father let out the house.

It is interesting that in five cases a property arrangement of some kind had taken place with the result that the child and the parent looking after it continued to live in the house. Lawyers had been consulted in three of them, and in half of all the cases involving owner-occupiers. What has emerged, therefore, is not necessarily a pattern dictated by legal advice although the outcomes follow the policies urged by courts in the case of divorced parents (but see p. 112) and suggests that similar policies might appropriately be adopted for non-married parents.[6]

What happened to the fathers? The four who had stayed in the house were still there at time of the interview. Of those who had departed, none were known to have remained in the owner-occupied sector. Two were renting, three were with their parents, one with friends, one was abroad and we lacked information on two.

Changes in family structure

Apart from these changes in material circumstances, these children might experience a reconstitution of the membership of the household in which they are living. It will be recalled that 15 per cent of the "never-together" children had acquired a stepparent (always a stepfather) since the birth, although three had already acquired one when they were born, making 22 per cent in all (p. 67). As regards the partnerships of their "outside" parent, comparison with the "never-together" group cannot be exact because that group contains "outside" parents who were partnered to someone other than the mother when the child was born. But if we include such existing partnerships for that group, the familial circumstances of the study children at time of interview in the two

---

[6] The Law Commission is expected to put forward suggestions for consideration during 1997.

Table 6.7: Parents with Partners at Time of Interview—Never-together and Former Cohabiting Parent Groups

	Never-together group		Former cohabiting parent group	
	Number n = 46	%	Number n = 51	%
Parent with whom child living	10*	22	18**	35
"Outside" parent	16***	35	22****	43

* Includes three where mother acquired partner before child's birth
** Includes two of the three fathers looking after the child.
*** Includes six where fathers had partners at time of the child's birth
**** Includes one who later separated and one who repartnered three times

groups is expressed in Table 6.7. This shows in how many cases the parent with whom the study child was living acquired (or already had) a partner and in how many cases the child's "outside" parent acquired (or already had) a partner. For some children, of course, both parents acquired a partner. In two cases in each group a parent had acquired two new partners.

On this information, parents in the "former cohabiting parent" group repartnered more frequently than those in the "never-together" group, though we must remember that the latter group included six parents who had previously been married to or had cohabited with one another before the child was born. To compare the propensity to acquire a partner, we would need to exclude from the "never-together" group in Table 6.6 the mother who was cohabiting with another man when the child was born and the six fathers who were living with another woman at that time. If this is done, the former cohabitants seem to acquire subsequent partners at a quite markedly higher rate than the parents in the "never-together" group. In both groups the "outside" parent, who generally[7] was not looking after any children, appears to acquire a partner slightly more readily than the parent who is looking after the children.

Two children experienced significant changes of an unusual kind. While none had moved permanently from one parent to another, two had moved out of the maternal home. One boy, now 16, had been evicted by his mother after causing trouble between her and her new partner. He lived briefly with his father, but they did not get on and his father's partner demanded that he leave. He was now in a hostel for the homeless. The second, aged 2, had been regularly visited by the father, but was taken into care by the local authority after his mother, an alcoholic with a history of assaulting the father (who was hiding from her), had set the family home on fire.

[7] However in three of the former cohabiting parent cases children were split between the parents.

As far as family *structure* is concerned, we should also remark that, at the time of the interview, twenty-four of the children had full siblings in the household, four had half-siblings in the household and six had half-siblings outside the household. Seven (14 per cent) had full siblings living elsewhere. These include the two cases just mentioned, but also three cases where the siblings had been "split" between the parents. This had not occurred at all in the case of the "never-together" group, where eleven children had full siblings and two had half-siblings, but all lived in the same household.

Parenting during cohabitation

Since in all these cases the parents had been living together when the child was born, we were able to ask for their assessments of the degree to which they collaborated as parents while they were together. We asked how far the parents shared responsibility for the day-to-day care of the child when it was under 5. This was reported in six out of fifty-one (12 per cent) of cases, five out of forty-three (12 per cent) by women respondents and by one of the eight (12 per cent) men respondents, so there appears to be no gender bias in the reporting. Although there will inevitably be some lack of precision over exactly how the idea of equal sharing of day-to-day responsibility is interpreted, it seems that these six cases are likely at least to represent circumstances where the parents perceived a high degree of collaboration between them regarding their care for the child.

Contact and relationships between parents

What, then, happened after separation? There was significantly more contact between the parents in this group in the period immediately after separation than there was between the parents shortly after the child's birth in the case of those who had never lived together. But the quality of the relationships was poorer (Table 6.8).

So, in all, thirty-nine out of fifty-one (76 per cent) of the former cohabiting parents were in contact after the separation. However, relationships between them were much worse than between the parents in the "never-together" group both at the time of the separation (or birth, in the case of the "never-togethers") and at interview. However, parents in both groups experienced a reduction of conflict over time. Although for the groups as a whole this involved primarily movement from a bad relationship to no relationship at all, rather than any increase in good relationships, we will see that where a parent retained contact with the child, the relationships between the parents

Table 6.8: Contact and Relationship Between Parents—Never-together and Former Cohabiting Parent Groups

(a) Contact between parents at time of birth/separation

	At least weekly %	Less frequent %	None %
Never-together group (n = 46)	38	22	40
Former cohabiting parent group (n = 51)	52	24	25

(b) Relationship between parents at birth/separation and at interview

	Good %	Neutral %	Bad %	No rel. %	Unknown %
At birth/separation					
Never-together group (n = 46)*	28	11	17	39	4
Former cohabiting parent group (n = 51)	25	8	45	22	0
At interview					
Never together group (n = 46)*	26	13	4	50	7
Former cohabiting parent group (n = 51)	24	27	14	35	0

* See Table 5.3, which gives the absolute numbers.

tended to improve over time (p. 96 below). Violence sometimes seemed to be in evidence. We did not ask about violence in general terms, as this would have been a particularly complex and sensitive topic in the context of the interviews we were conducting, but we did ask whether those who had consulted a lawyer had raised the question of personal protection. Two women and a man had done this. In another two cases, the respondents had mentioned violence in the context of contact by the father, and we have already referred to the man who was in hiding from his arsonist former partner (p. 92). We can therefore say that violence seemed to have occurred in not less than 12 per cent of cases, but we cannot be sure it was not more frequent. We found no references to violence in the "never-together" group, but as we have noted, solicitors were consulted in only two cases in that group.

On the other hand, equal sharing of parental care was associated with good relationships before and after separation; four of the six experienced good relationships at separation, though one subsequently declined to "no relationship", and four had good relationships at interview. None said the relationship was bad at any point.

Contact between parents and children

General comparison with "never-together" group

What, then, of contact between the "outside" parents and the children? We divided this into cases where it continued uninterrupted from the separation until the interview ("continuing contact"); cases where it stopped at separation and never resumed ("no contact ever"); "irregular contact" cases where contact was infrequent but sufficiently maintained that we could not say there was no commitment at all (for example, the father who for 15 years saw the child about three times a year "when sober", with the help of his new partner; or the father being in prison); cases where it had continued after separation but later stopped ("contact ended") and cases where it had stopped at separation but resumed later: "contact restarted". The overall position is shown in Table 6.9.

Table 6.9: Contact Between Parents and Children—Never-together and Former Cohabiting Parent Groups

Contact	Former cohabiting parent group n = 51 %	Never-together group n = 46 %
Continuing contact	45	35
No contact	14	39
False starts	0	13
Interrupted contact/contact ended	24	13
Irregular contact	10	0
Contact restarted	6	0

We found that ten out of fifty-one (20 per cent) of the children were not in contact during the period immediately after the separation. This compares with 39 per cent of the "never-together" group. But these children in the "never-together" group never subsequently made contact, whereas three (6 per cent) of the present group restarted it later. The "irregular" section among the former cohabiting parents was similar to the "false starts" of the "never-together" group, showing low-level interest, but sustaining it for longer. If these are excluded, the overall picture is that 69 per cent of the former cohabiting parents continued contact with the child immediately after the separation compared to 48 per cent of the "never-together" group who maintained contact with the child after its birth, but that 51 per cent (including the "re-starts") of the former and 35 per cent of the latter were in committed, continuing contact at the time of interview.

Contact and relationships between parents

Although the former cohabitants had worse relationships with each other than the parents in the "never-together" group, it appears that this did not significantly impede contact between the child and the other parent at the time of the separation. In fact, using a more refined measure of parental relationships, we can see that where parents remained in contact, their relationships frequently improved over time. Eleven out of twenty-three (48 per cent) reported actual improvements (Table 6:10). Only three reported a worsening of the relationship, and for the rest the relationship either remained the same or moved to a "no relationship" description. It was similar, but slightly less marked, for the "never-together" group, where five out of sixteen (31 per cent) of the parents who kept contact with the child reported improved relationships with the other parent. All the others reported no change in the relationship except one where it declined from "very good" to "fairly good" and two where bad relationships dissolved into no relationships.

Table 6.10: Improved Relationships Between Parents in Contact over Time—Never-together and Former Cohabiting Parent Groups

State of relationship	Cohabiting parent group Total in contact = 23 No.	Never-together group Total in contact = 16 No.
Very bad to neutral	2	1
Bad to very good	1	0
Fairly bad to neutral	3	1
Fairly bad to fairly good	1	0
No relationship to fairly good	1	0
Neutral to fairly good	0	1
Fairly good to very good	3	1
Good to very good	0	1
Total	11	5

We found no case, however, where either parent claimed that joint decisions between them were being made in matters concerning the child's upbringing.

As in the case of the "never-together" group, where parents were never in contact with the child, the parental relationship was almost always reported as being non-existent (five out of seven: 71 per cent) and where it ended or was irregular, the relationships were usually reported to be bad at separation (eleven out of seventeen: 65 per cent). But, over time, apart from two cases where the relationships remained bad, these changed either to a neutral relationship or no relationship at all by the time of the interview.

Ages of children and time since separation

The ages of the sixteen children in the "never-together" group who retained contact with the outside parent, and therefore the period of time for which the contact had continued, were quite low. One half were under 3. Only one was over 10. In the twenty-three cases in the former cohabiting parent group where contact had been continuously maintained, this had gone on for less than three years in twelve out of twenty-three (52 per cent) of the cases and, although three had persisted for over ten years, there is no real difference in the periods of time for which contact had been going on between the two groups.

The ages of the children at the time of the separation affected the likelihood of contact continuing (Table 6.11).

Table 6.11: Ages of Children at Separation—Former Cohabiting Parent Group

Age of child	Continuing contact	No contact	Irregular contact	Contact ended	Contact restarted	All
Under 2	8	5	3	6	1	23
2–4	9	1	1	6	0	17
5–6	1	0	2	0	1	4
7–10	5	0	0	0	1	6
Over 10	0	1	0	0	0	1
Totals	23	7	6	12	3	51

It is notable that the older the children were at separation the more likely they were to remain in continuous contact with the "outside" parent. Contact continued for nine out of twenty-four (37 per cent) of the under-2s (if we include the restart it becomes 42 per cent) but never started, became irregular or stopped for fourteen out of twenty-four (58 per cent) of them. The children aged 2 to 4 fared a little better, eight out of sixteen (50 per cent) keeping contact with the "outside" parent and the other half losing it. Six out of eleven (54 per cent) of the over-5s kept contact (73 per cent if we add the restarts), with contact being lost or becoming irregular for three out of eleven (27 per cent).

Distance the "outside" parent lived from child

As in the case of the "never-together" group, those in contact are more likely to be living near to the child than the those whose contact ended or who were never in contact. But, as for that group, merely being close by by no means assured contact; twelve out of thirty (40 per cent) of the outside parents who were living within ten miles of the child exercised no or only irregular contact (Table 6.12).

Table 6.12: Distance at which "Outside" Parent Lives from Child—Former Cohabiting Parent Group

Distance from child	Continuing contact	No contact	Irregular contact	Contact ended	Contact restarted	All
Under 10 miles	16	2	5	5	2	30
Over 10 miles	6	4	1	7	1	19
Unknown	1	1	0	0	0	2
Totals	23	7	6	12	3	51

Table 6.13: Contact and Employment—Former Cohabiting Parent Group

Work status of father	Continuing contact	No contact	Irregular contact	Contact ended	Contact restarted	All
Full-time	13	3	2	7	2	27
Unemployed	9	2	2	4	1	18
Unknown	0	1	2	0	0	3
Totals	22	6	6	11	3	48

Contact, employment and financial support

Information about the employment status of the father was better for this group than for the "never-together" group, and this is presented in Table 6.13. This states his employment position at the time of the separation and excludes the three cases where the mother was the outside parent.

There seems to be no association between employment status at time of separation and the exercise of contact. Nearly half of all fathers were in contact, and so were nearly half the fathers in full-time work, while the other half either were not in contact or had problems over it. Similarly, half of the men who were unemployed at the time of separation maintained contact, while the other half experienced various difficulties over it.

However, even if fathers were in full-time work, and exercising contact, the incidence of financial support was very low (Table 6.14). Once again the fathers who were looking after children are excluded.

The Child Support Agency was known to be have approached only a minority of the fathers. It did so in only ten of the thirty-nine cases where support had not been paid or was being paid irregularly.

Generally, payment of support was poor: there was none being paid in thirty-three out of forty-eight (69 per cent) of cases. In fifteen cases (31 per cent) the father was known to be unemployed, sick or in a training scheme. But in fifteen out of forty-eight (31 per cent) of cases he was known to be

Table 6.14: Contact and Financial Support—Former Cohabiting Parent Group

(a) Financial support

Support paid	Continuing contact	No contact	Irregular contact	Contact ended	Contact restarted	All
Yes	5*	0	0	2+	1	8
Irregular	2	1	2	2	0	7
No	15	5	4	7	2**	33
Totals	22	6	6	11	3	48++

(b) Child Support Agency approach to father

CSA approach	Continuing contact	No contact	Irregular contact	Contact ended	Contact restarted	All
Yes	8	3	2	4	1	18
No or unknown	14	3	4	7	2	30
Totals	22	6	6	11	3	48

* Includes one "in kind"
+ One of £1 per week to DSS; one of £21 per week when in work
** Includes one refusal by mother to accept
++ Excludes 3 custodial fathers

employed full-time. Why should a full-time worker not pay? Possible reasons appear in Table 6.15. (There was insufficient information in five cases).

There appeared to be a similar proportion of cases in this group (twenty-five out of thirty-five: 71 per cent) as among the "never-together" group (68 per cent) where there appeared to be some plausible reason why financial support was not being paid by the father to the child. No unemployed man was paying support and of the twenty repartnered fathers, eighteen were not paying or were paying irregularly, of whom seven were in full-time work. Three of these, however, had made some kind of property arrangement involving the house, and one said the mother refused to accept payments. Of the other two, only one was paying full support and the other was giving support "in kind". As for the "never-together" group, repartnership turned out to be a strong factor associated with non-payment of support.

Contact and repartnering
The relationship between contact and repartnering is shown in Table 6.16, which also breaks the study children into groups according to their age *at separation*.

The strong association between repartnering and the exercise of contact appears from the fact that in fourteen out of twenty-three (61 per cent) of cases where contact continued, neither party had re-partnered, whereas either

Table 6.15: Possible Reasons for Non-payment of Support—Former Cohabiting Parents Group

Possible reasons	Number
Unemployed	15
Working full-time BUT	
Father repartnered	1
Mother repartnered	3
Both repartnered	2
Admitted collusion	1
Mother refused to accept	1
Child in care	1
House transfer in lieu	1
No reason known and father reported	
to be in full-time work	5
Sub-total	30
Insufficient information	5
Total	35

or both parents had repartnered in nineteen out of twenty-five (76 per cent) of the "no contact" cases. In all, contact continued in fourteen out of seventeen (82 per cent) of cases where neither repartnered. In the case of the "never-together" group, not having a partner seemed to be an important condition for contact to continue (88 per cent of those in continuing contact had neither a pre-existing nor subsequent partner) but did not seem to make its continuation so likely as in the case of the former cohabitants (54 per cent of those where neither had a partner kept in contact) (see p. 76 above).

However, we saw (p. 97) that the continuation of contact was also strongly associated with the age of the child at the time of the separation. That is, the older the child was at separation the more likely it was that contact would continue. Was this a sufficiently strong factor to overcome the apparently adverse effect which repartnering had on contact? It is difficult to tell. Table 6.16 shows that contact was continued with only eight out of twenty-three (35 per cent) of all children under 2 at separation, but with six out of eight (75 per cent) of children under 2 whose parents had not repartnered. So even where the child was under 2, children without repartnered parents were more likely to keep contact. However, this result might be influenced by the fact that in our sample parents who separated before the child was 2 were slightly over-represented among those who were interviewed within two years of the separation, and are therefore less likely to have repartnered anyway (Table 6.17). But in the case of children over 2 at separation, the parents were more likely to have been interviewed more than two years after the separation. Fifteen out of twenty-eight (54 per cent) of all these children were still in

Table 6.16: Contact and Repartnering According to Age of Child at Separation—Formerly Cohabiting Parent Group

Age groups	Contact continuing	No contact*	Restart	Totals
Children under 2				
"Outside" p'nt only r'ptd	1	3	0	4
"Caring" p'nt only r'ptd	0	3	0	3
Both parents r'ptd	0	3	1	4
Neither parent r'ptd	6	2	0	8
Not known	1	3	0	4
Sub-total	8	14	1	23
Children 2–4				
"Outside" p'nt only r'ptd	3	4	0	7
"Caring" p'nt only r'ptd	2	2	0	4
Both parents r'ptd	0	1	0	1
Neither parent r'ptd	4**	0	0	4
Not known	0	1	0	1
Sub-total	9	8	0	17
Children 5–6				
"Outside" p'nt only r'ptd	0	1	0	1
"Caring" p'nt only r'ptd	1	0	0	1
Both parents r'ptd	0	1	0	1
Neither parent r'ptd	0	0	1	1
Not known	0	0	0	0
Sub-total	1	2	1	4
Children 7–10				
"Outside" p'nt only r'ptd	1	0	0	1
"Caring" p'nt only r'ptd	0	0	0	0
Both parents r'ptd	0	0	0	0
Neither parent r'ptd	4**	0	0	4
Not known	0	0	0	0
Sub-total	5	0	0	5
Children over 10				
"Outside" p'nt only r'ptd	0	0	0	0
"Caring" p'nt only r'ptd	0	1	0	1
Both parents r'ptd	0	0	1	1
Neither parent r'ptd	0	0	0	0
Not known	0	0	0	0
Sub-total	0	1	1	2
Totals	23	25	3	51

Table 6.17: Length of Time Between Separation and Interview for All Children and Children Under and Over 2 at Separation

Age of child	Time since interview (years)				
	Under 2	2–4	5–6	7–9	Over 10
Under 2 (n = 24) Cum %	37	58	75	79	100
Over 2 (n = 27) Cum %	15	55	81	85	100
All (n = 51) Cum %	25	56	78	82	100

contact with the outside parent at time of interview. But this was true with respect to only seven out of eighteen (38 per cent) of cases where one or both of the parents had repartnered. Where neither had repartnered, contact was retained in eight out of nine (89 per cent) of cases. So for older children the repartnering factor seems strong, but it must be recognized that the numbers of cases in this group where the parents left older children was very small. We recall that for the "never-together" group, partnering by the outside parent with another adult appeared to be a significant obstacle to contact. This might also be true for the formerly cohabiting parents, though the exercise of contact could also have been influenced by the age of the child at separation.[8]

Another feature which might assist contact is the exercise during the cohabitation of an equal sharing of responsibility for the child. We saw that this was reported in six cases. It seems that this *may* help to facilitate contact, because in five out of six (83 per cent) of cases where it was exercised contact was never lost, and that occurred in only twenty-three out of fifty-one (45 per cent) of all the cases. However, it cannot be shown to have a stronger impact on contact than repartnering because it occurred only in cases where children were under 4 at separation, and in five of the six cases where contact continued, neither parent repartnered.

"Outside" parents repartnered slightly more often than parents with the study child (18:14). However, whether it was the "outside" or "caring" parent who repartnered seemed to be irrelevant as regards the child's likelihood to retain contact.

The post-marital cohabitants

We referred earlier to the distinction between the post-marital cohabitants and the never-married cohabitants. Although the number of post-marital cohabitants was small (six women and one man), we excluded them from some of our comparisons in case they displayed markedly different characteristics from the others. Indeed, they did seem to form a somewhat older sub-group.

---

[8] For a statistical comment, see Methodological Appendix.

However, it turned out that they were little different from the rest. For example, four out of seven (57 per cent) of the fathers were in full-time work at the time of the separation, exactly the same proportion as the others. However, only one of the women was unemployed at that time, but two acquired part-time work by the time of interview. The payment of maintenance was hardly better; only two paid, and one did so irregularly. None of them had practised equal sharing of parental responsibility. Their relationships at the time of separation were slightly better than for the group as a whole, four out of seven saying they were fairly good. One feature about this sub-group is interesting. The children were slightly older at the time of separation than for the group as a whole: five out of seven (57 per cent) were over 5, compared to 22 per cent for the whole group. We are reluctant to read anything into these figures because of the small cells involved, though they raise the question whether cohabitations producing children which break down may persist for longer if they have been entered into after a marriage than if neither party has been previously married.

TWO CASE STUDIES

Two case studies will help to provide a more vivid context for our conclusions about this group of our sample.

Christine
Christine was 2 when her mother, Wendy (who was now aged 30), was interviewed. George, Christine's father, had moved into Wendy's house and was living there when Christine was born. However, the parents separated when Christine was one. Neither parent had any other children. Although they lived together, Wendy and George did not share their lives fully. Both were working, she part-time and he full-time, but she lived mainly on her own earnings of about £12,000. Things in fact changed little when George left and went to live with his parents a short distance from Wendy's home. She continued to work and indeed to see or speak to George several times a week. But his interest in Christine was fading. Although he saw her about once a month for some time, now he either doesn't turn up at the times agreed or comes around when she is in bed. He has lost his job and gives no financial assistance to Wendy, but had never done so. Wendy says that, although their relationship was initially fairly bad after they separated, there was now no real relationship at all. Neither has formed any new partnership. They have merely drifted apart, as parents, but it seems that George was never strongly involved as a parent at all. They have gone through this period of their lives without feeling the need to obtain any professional advice. It seems unlikely that Christine will develop any relationship with George, especially if he acquires a new partner later on.

Gary

Gary is 13. His mother, Cynthia (now 31) was living with his father, Donald, in local authority rented accommodation when he was born, but they separated shortly afterwards, when Gary was one. That was in 1981. Donald was unemployed at the time. He continued to see Gary, however, and this contact increased even though Cynthia subsequently lived with William for two years, and had two children by him. Donald, who has not acquired a new partner, is now living just around the corner and sees Gary frequently. Donald now has a full-time job, but gave no financial support to Gary, even though Cynthia is living on income support. But Donald's mother, who is very close to Gary, buys him things. Cynthia and Donald have a good relationship.

CONCLUSIONS

It must be remembered that these parents operated only within a limited legal framework. Because they had not been married to each other, the divorce jurisdiction was unavailable to them and neither owed a legal obligation to support the other. However, each parent was under a duty to support the child financially, and came within the remit of the Child Support Scheme.

We discovered that a court order for child maintenance existed in ten out of fifty-one (20 per cent) of cases, though there was regular compliance in only four cases. After April 1993 the courts lost their jurisdiction to make such orders except in exceptional cases (see pp. 38–9), and the Child Support Agency had been in contact with twenty-three out of fifty-one (45 per cent) of fathers. However, only four orders had been made, of which only two were paid regularly (in one case, possibly because the CSA assessment was for less than the prior court order). In one case the man thought he need not pay because the child was in foster care as the mother was receiving psychiatric treatment. Eight parents said they had an "informal" arrangement, and this was complied with regularly in five cases, a slightly higher rate of compliance than for the court orders. One mother said she was being mainly supported by her former partner.

If we try to evaluate the overall social capital brought to these children by the fact that their fathers had been living (unmarried) with their mothers when they were born, the results are not impressive. It is true that the family was more likely to live in owner-occupied homes than the "never-together" group (27 per cent against 10 per cent), and to enjoy a higher household income. But there was high unemployment (57 per cent of fathers) and reliance on benefits (48 per cent). The relationships seemed fragile. Nearly half of them had broken up when the study child was under 2, and four-fifths before the child was 5. After separation, three-quarters of the fathers gave no financial support, and at interview only half were in contact with the children. The proportion of mothers in employment actually dropped after the separation, which might have adverse long-term consequences for the children, especially girls, according to Kiernan's (1996) account (p. 58). There were some gains. 64 per cent of those few who had been in the owner-occupied sector were still there when interviewed. They were better off, and there was marginally more contact, than was the case for the "never-togethers". But there was also some recorded violence.

Of course, we have surveyed only those cohabitations which broke down. But it seems that where this does happen the longer-term benefits for most of the children involved arising from the fact that their parents did live together are very questionable. Unlike the children in the "never-together" group, they may have suffered the negative effects of separation, but the degree of ongoing parental support from the outside parent after separation was low. We now need to see how this compares to the children whose parents had been married before they broke up.

7

Children Whose Parents Had Married

We now turn to our final, and largest, group: children whose parents had not only been living together when the child was born but had been doing so within the formal relationship of marriage. Although the group includes parents who were separated as well as those who were divorced we will call it, for convenience, the "formerly married parents" group. The literature on children brought up in one-parent families (see Chapter 4) tends to contrast the general under-achievement and disadvantages of these children with the happier position of children of two-parent families. In this context, the expression "two-parent" normally implies that the parents are married. However, there are also many studies, reviewed in Chapter 4, which testify to the problems these children face if the two-parent unit breaks apart. We wished to examine how far the post-divorce circumstances of these children compared to the post-separation circumstances of children whose parents had cohabited but not married, and also to the familial circumstances of children who never lived together with both their parents.

CHARACTERISTICS OF THIS GROUP

One hundred and three women and forty-nine men (total = 152) who had been married to each other were interviewed. One hundred of the women and seven of the fathers who were interviewed had the study child living with them. In all, ten (7 per cent) children were living with their father, and one with the father's relatives. We cannot therefore assume that the "outside" parent is the father, and as in the previous chapter, we will use the expressions "outside" and "caring" parents to describe the positions of these two parents vis-a-vis the study child.

Nor can we assume that all these parents had divorced the other, although, as stated above, we call this group the "formerly married parents". This must be taken into account when we compare our sample to the national data presented in the *General Household Survey* (GHS). In order to do this we need to extract from our sample those parents who correspond to the "lone mothers" in the GHS. The GHS data state that in 1994 33 per cent of lone mothers in Great Britain had been divorced and that 24 per cent were separated (making 57 per cent who had been married); 38 per cent are described as "single" and 5 per cent as "widowed".[1] Of course widowed parents are excluded from our study. Our sample was not comprised solely of lone parents, however, as many had acquired a partner, or a new partner, at the time of interview. However, if we exclude those, we will have a subset of lone parents. There were 188 women in the whole sample, of whom 183 were looking after the child. A total of forty-nine of these women had partners, leaving 134 living alone with the child. These were our lone mothers. Of them, 68 out of 134 (51 per cent) were formerly married women living alone with the child. This is close to the 57 per cent of lone mothers who on the GHS figures were once married. Indeed, if we exclude from our sixty-eight once-married lone mothers the twenty-three who had not yet divorced we have 45 out of 134 (34 per cent) who had been divorced, an almost identical proportion to that in the GHS. Similarly, the 23 out of 134 (17 per cent) married but separated mothers is consistent with the 24 per cent in the GHS survey.[2]

The remainder of lone mothers in the GHS (excluding widows) are described as "single" (38 per cent), but these must include mothers who had at some time lived with the father without marrying him. It is therefore reasonable to see this GHS category as corresponding to those non-repartnered mothers in both our "never-together" and "former cohabiting parent" groups. These amount to 49 per cent of our sample, slightly higher than the GHS proportion, but it must be remembered that the "never-together" group is augmented by four out of forty-six (9 per cent) mothers who had been married previously, though not to the child's father, and who would therefore be counted as divorced or separated in the GHS data set and not as "single" parents. Given these adjustments, the composition of the lone mothers in our sample is very similar to that in the GHS population.

If we look at the ages of the children of lone mothers in the different groups in our study at time of interview, they turn out as shown in Table 7.1.

The proportions for the children of the separated and divorced lone mothers in our sample closely track those given by Haskey (1993: Table 5) from national data sets. He gives the following age distribution. Separated lone mothers: age 0–4 (28 per cent); age 5–9 (35 per cent); over 10 (31 per cent). Divorced lone mothers: age 0–4 (15 per cent); age 5–9 (30 per cent); over 10 (46 per cent). Single lone mothers: age 0–4 (63 per cent); age 5–9 (25 per cent); over 10 (11 per cent). Haskey's figures for single mothers diverge from ours for the "never-together" and "former cohabiting parent" groups. However, within those two groups are included a number of women who had already been married to the father (but had left him before the child had been born) or had been married to another man. These would have been excluded from

---

[1] *General Household Survey 1994*, Table 2.13. See also Burghes with Brown (1995: 5).

[2] Our proportions of various types of lone parent families are also consistent with those found by Marsh, Ford and Finlayson (1997: Table 1.1. and 4–5).

Table 7.1: Ages of Children of Lone Mothers

Group	0–4 %	5–9 %	Over 10 %
Never-together (n=37)	54	35	11
Former cohabiting (n=30)	43	33	23
Never-together and former cohabiting added (n=67)	49	34	16
Separated (n=25)	24	40	36
Divorced (n=36)	14	30	55

Haskey's "single" lone mothers. In fact, the significantly higher proportion of older children of the divorced and separated lone mothers is evident in both ours and Haskey's data.

The ages of the formerly married mothers were higher than in the other groups. Only 16 per cent were under 30 at the time of the interview compared to 46 per cent of the former cohabitants and 68 per cent of the mothers in the "never-together" group. This is consistent with Haskey's (1993: Table 6) data showing that "single" lone-mother households are headed by much younger women than separated and divorced lone-mother households.

Finally, we need to consider the time which had elapsed between separation and interview. Table 7.2 sets this out for our three groups (in the case of the "never-together" group the time given is that since the birth of the child). It appears that there is little variation between them which could adversely affect comparisons between the groups regarding events after the separation (or birth).

Table 7.2: Years Between Birth/Separation and Interview—All Groups

Years	Never-together group n = 46 %	Former cohabiting parents n = 51 %	Formerly married parents n = 152 %
0–2	24	25	20
2–4	26	31	32
5–6	24	20	19
7–10	20	6	16
Over 10	6	18	13

CHARACTERISTICS OF THE FAMILY OF ORIGIN OF THE CHILDREN

We now compare the material resources into which the children of the formerly married parents were born with those of the other groups. It will become quickly apparent that this group enjoys many advantages over the others.

Housing

The housing status of our three groups at the time of separation (or birth of the child, in the case of the "never-together" group) is presented in Table 7.3.

Table 7.3: Housing Status at Birth/Separation—All Groups

Status	Never-together group n = 46 %	Former cohabiting parent group n = 51 %	Formerly married group n = 152 %
Owner-occupation	9	25	58
Renting	22	75	38
At home	46	0	0
Other	19	0	4

Kiernan and Estaugh (1993: 13), using 1989 GHS data, give 39 per cent of cohabitants with children as living in owner-occupation compared to 72 per cent of married people who have children. We also show fewer of the former cohabitants in owner-occupation than the married, but both our groups display considerably less owner-occupation than exists for the general population of cohabitants and married people with children. However, ours is a sub-set of that population comprising those among it who experienced separation. Although the depression in the housing market and high unemployment have weakened the security formerly offered by owner-occupation, these figures are consistent with the suggestion made in the previous chapter that the stability of unmarried cohabitation, just as for married cohabitation, is weaker for couples who enjoy less material security. As we will immediately see, this is also shown in other measures of economic well-being.

Employment and income

We saw that former cohabiting fathers were more likely to be in employment prior to the separation than the fathers in the "never-together" group. This was still at a lower rate than non-married fathers reported by Kiernan and Estaugh (1993) who are still living with their partners. Many more of the formerly married fathers were employed before separation than the former cohabitants: 117 out of 152 (77 per cent) were in full-time work as against 55 per cent of the former cohabitants. Twenty-five out of 152 (16 per cent) were unemployed, compared to 39 per cent of the latter. Although higher than the former cohabiting fathers, this employment rate is lower than the 93 per cent for all married fathers with dependent children given by Kiernan and Estaugh (1993: 15) for 1989, which is a reasonable year for comparison because most of the separations in our group had taken place at various points within the past ten years (Table 7.2). However, it is consistent with the established evidence that marital breakdown is associated with instability of employment (see p. 88).

The women respondents (n=103) reported on their own employment situation at the time of the separation. 17 per cent were in full-time employment and 31 per cent were working part-time; thus 48 per cent were earning. This compares to 7 per cent of the mothers in the "never-together" group who were employed at the time of the child's birth and the 41 per cent of former cohabitants (17 per cent full-time, 24 per cent part-time). There was therefore very little difference in employment patterns between the former cohabiting *mothers* and the formerly married mothers. Nor were they very different from the extent of employment for actually cohabiting and married women with dependent children in 1989 reported by Kiernan and Estaugh (1993: 15): 43 per cent of the former were working and 53 per cent of the latter.

Nor was there much difference between these two groups as regards the mothers' educational qualifications (Table 7.4). This Table also shows, in brackets, the equivalent percentages for mothers aged between 20 and 34 for 1989 reported by Kiernan and Estaugh (1993: 13).

Table 7.4: Educational Qualifications of Mothers—All Groups

Qualification	Never-together group n = 41 %	Former cohabiting parent group n = 43 %	Formerly married parent group n = 103 %
No qualification	40	37(43)	32(25)
GCE/GCSE/O level	47	45(24)	44(34)
Vocational	2	10(3)	8(20)
A levels	2	8(11)	6(7)
Degree or diploma	9	13(9)	11(14)

Hence with respect to the employment practice and educational qualifications of mothers, women who have exited from unmarried or married cohabitation have very similar profiles to those who are still living in such unions. The difference between those who have separated and the whole populations of married and non-married cohabitants seems to lie in the circumstances of the *fathers*, particularly with regard to their employment status.

Consistent with the higher incidence of men's employment in the married households, the household income of that group was above that of the others

(Table 6.5). It was under £6,000 p.a. for only 17 per cent, compared with 87 per cent for the "never-togethers" and 40 per cent for the former cohabitants; and 25 per cent received over £16,000, compared to only 6 per cent of the former cohabitants and none of the "never-togethers". Benefits were reported as having been the main source of income before separation in 20 out of 150 (13 per cent) cases, contrasting strongly with 37 per cent in the case of the former cohabitants and 93 per cent of the mothers in the "never-together" group. None of this is surprising, given the difference in the fathers' employment patterns discussed above.

Table 7.5: Household Incomes at Child's Birth/Before Separation—All Groups

Income	Never-together group n = 23* Cum %	Former cohabiting parent group n = 46** Cum %	Formerly married group n = 133*** Cum %
Under £6,000	87	39	17
£6,001 to £10,000	13	67	41
£10,001 to £15,000	0	91	75
Over £15,000	100	100	100

* Only those living independently of their parents.
** See Table 6.6(c).
*** Information unavailable in 19 cases.

Although the formerly married parents were clearly better off than the other groups at the time of separation, they are still less well off than most married people with children. Kiernan and Estaugh (1993: 17), on the basis of the *General Household Survey 1989* data, give only 20 per cent of married couples with children as having a weekly gross household income of under £200 (about £10,000 p.a.), whereas 58 per cent of our formerly married parents would fall within that category. This is consistent with the evidence of an association between marriage breakdown and relative economic hardship.

CHANGES IN FAMILY CIRCUMSTANCES

Thus far, our findings about the formerly married group mainly confirm what is already known. That is, that marriage breakdown is associated with relative economic and material adversity, though we have shown that this is also true for the breakdown of non-marital cohabitations. Our main concern, however, is with what happened after the parents separated.

Housing changes

We wished to track the longer-term housing situation for the children after the separation. In the case of the owner-occupiers, we give the housing outcome at time of interview for those mothers who were looking after the study child. In 40 out of eighty-three (48 per cent) of cases the mother and child were still in the house, which had always (except once) been in joint names. This was a marked increase on the proportion of occasions when the mother and child remained in the house shown in our earlier study which had been based on people who divorced during the 1970s (Eekelaar and Maclean (1984: 214)). Then the wife stayed in only 26 per cent of cases. However, the proportion of cases where the father stayed was almost identical: 24 per cent in the 1970s and 25 per cent in the present study. Only two of the houses had been in his name; all the rest were in joint names. In one case he was looking after a child in a split custody arrangement. The house was sold in fewer cases than in the earlier study: now 37 per cent; previously 46 per cent. This may reflect the change from the more fluid housing market of the 1970s. It seems that the result of fewer sales has been an increase in the continued occupation of the home by the mother and the children. Nevertheless, the study child still moved in forty-three out of eighty-three (52 per cent) of cases. A higher proportion of children of former cohabitants stayed on in the house (six out of nine: 67 per cent), but the figures are too small for clear comparisons to be made.

Table 7.6 shows where the mother moved to in the 43 cases where she and the child left the home. It will be seen that the majority of the women were now in the rented sector, mostly without a new partner.

The fathers who left the home fared rather worse than the mothers and children. Table 7.7 shows where they were living at the time of interview. If we compare Tables 7.6 and 7.7, we find that at time of interview 40 per cent

Table 7.6: Mother and Child's Housing at Interview (Excluding Cases where they Stayed in the Family Home)—Formerly Married Parent Group

Housing	Number
With relatives	3
Renting alone	15
Renting with new partner	2
Owner-occupied alone	7
Owner-occupied with new partner	12
About to move	1
Unclear	3
Total	43

Table 7.7: Fathers' Housing at Interview (Excluding Fathers who Stayed in the Home)— Formerly Married Parent Group

Housing	Number
Rented	14
Rented with new partner	4
Owner occupied	8
Owner occupied with new partner	11
With relatives	12
With friends	2
In lodgings	1
In army	2
In police accommodation	1
Unclear	12
Total	67

of mothers who left the home were renting compared to 37 per cent of fathers; 44 per cent of mothers had remained in the owner-occupied sector compared to 28 per cent of fathers, and that 7 per cent of mothers were with relatives compared to 20 per cent of fathers who were with relatives or friends. The mothers are greatly helped by repartnering in remaining in owner-occupation, whereas many fathers whose former wives stay on in the family home take some considerable time to return into that sector.

The former cohabiting fathers who had been in owner-occupation followed similar paths after the separation (see p. 91).

By contrast with the owner-occupiers, where the parents were living in rented accommodation, only 23 per cent of children moved at the time of separation. This is very close to the 21 per cent who moved from local authority rented accommodation in our earlier study (Eekelaar and Maclean (1984: 214), but is slightly lower than the children of former cohabitants in the present study, of whom 35 per cent moved from rented accommodation.

Income and employment

We observed in the previous chapter that, after plummeting in the immediate aftermath of the separation, by the time of interview the financial position of the former cohabitants had generally recovered to almost the same level it had been before the separation. Nevertheless, a large number (64 per cent) still relied on social security as the main income source; new partners made only a modest contribution to their new income, and mothers as a whole had fewer jobs, though a larger proportion worked full-time. How do the formerly

Table 7.8: Employment Changes of Mothers over Time—Former Cohabiting and Formerly Married Parent Groups

(a) Former cohabiting parent group

	Before separation	At interview	
		All mothers	Non-repartnered mother
	n = 51	n = 51	n = 40
	%	%	%
Full-time	16	16	20
Part-time	20	9	10
Unemployed	57	61	57
Full-time ed.	2	4	5
Sick	2	2	2
Unclear	2	6	5

(b) Formerly married parent group*

	Before separation	At interview	
		All mothers	Non-repartnered mother
	n = 152	n = 140*	n = 80*
	%	%	%
Full-time	18	23	17
Part-time	30	24	22
Unemployed	49	45	56
Full-time ed.	0	2	1
Sick	1	1	1
Unclear	2	6	1

* Information about mothers with children only.

married parents compare? Table 7.8 includes the relevant table from the previous chapter (Table 6.6) for ease of reference.

By time of interview, the former cohabiting mothers were less likely to be employed than before the separation; but the formerly married mothers were slightly more likely to be employed. This was mostly due to a sharp drop in part-time working by the former cohabitants. Non-repartnered formerly married parents were less likely to be employed at interview than the formerly married mothers as a whole, but were slightly more likely to be employed than the non-repartnered former cohabitants, mostly because a larger proportion worked part-time. In both cases the proportion of lone mothers who were not in paid work was high: 61 per cent of the former cohabitants and 45 per cent of the formerly married mothers. But the higher incidence of unemployment among the former cohabitants is marked. However, in neither case is the incidence of unemployment as high as for the mothers in the "never-together"

Table 7.9: Income Levels of Mothers—All Groups

(a) Never-together group*

	Income of mothers at time of interview (n = 42)
	Cum %
Under £4,000	33
£4,001–£6,000	63
£6,001–£8,000	84
Over £8,000	100

(b) Former cohabiting parent group**
Income levels over time: showing mothers' incomes

	Before separation n = 46 Cum %	After separation n = 40 Cum %	At interview n = 41 Cum %
Under £4,000	19	55	15
£4,001 to £6,000	39	80	51
£6,001 to £8,000	56	85	68
£8,001 to £10,000	67	90	76
£10,001 to £12,000	74	90	80
£12,001 to £15,000	91	97	93
Over £15,000	100	100	100

(c) Formerly married parent group
Income levels over time: showing mothers' incomes

	All mothers before separation n = 133+ Cum %	Mothers looking after child After separation n = 90++ Cum %	At interview n = 99+++ Cum %
Under £4,000	5	33	8
£4,001 to £6,000	17	62	41
£6,001 to £8,000	31	78	59
£8,001 to £10,000	41	85	65
£10,001 to £12,000	49	88	71
£12,001 to £15,000	62	92	77
£15,001 to £18,000	75	95	84
Over £18,000	100	100	100

* See p. 68.
** See Table 6.6(c).
+ Information unavailable in 19 cases.
++ Information from women with children only; incomplete in 10 cases.
+++ Information from women with children only; incomplete in 4 cases.

group, where 82 per cent were not employed. Marsh, Ford and Finlayson (1997: Table 4.1) report similar differentials between their groups.[3]

Tables 7.9 and 7.10 compare the incomes of all groups of parents over time. The inferior financial position of the mothers in the "never-together" group appears clearly. We can also see that, while the formerly married mothers started from a much higher income level before the separation than the former cohabitants, both groups suffered a severe drop in income shortly after the separation. However, whereas by the time of the interview the former cohabitants had almost (but not quite) recovered their pre-separation level, the formerly married were a long way from returning to theirs. Indeed, from the moment of separation, the income profile of the formerly married mothers with children falls to a level only slightly higher than that of the formerly cohabiting mothers.[4]

Despite the similarity in income levels between these two groups at the time of interview, the sources of that income varied slightly, as is seen from Table 7.10. A slightly higher proportion of former cohabitants relied on social security payments as the main source of income, and rather more formerly married mothers relied on their new partner. But these differences, as we have seen, did not significantly affect the comparison of their overall household income levels. The extent to which the households were relying on the mothers' earnings was almost the same in each group.

It may be of interest to compare the income levels of the formerly married mothers with the fathers in that group. Table 7.11 compares the income levels declared by fathers after the separation and at interview with the levels of the whole group before the separation. It will be seen that, although a slightly larger proportion received under £6,000 than before the separation, the increase is not nearly so great as for the mothers, and at the higher levels there is very little difference, especially at the time of interview, from their position before separation.

Table 7.12 comprises only the fathers who were looking after children, either as sole custodial father or by looking after one child under a split custodial arrangement. Since there were only nine men in this category, one of whom was sick at time of interview, the figures must be regarded as suggestive only. They show that these fathers, at any rate, did experience a decline of income after separation, though not as great as the mothers did, especially in the middle-income levels. However there did seem to be a noticeable drop in the proportion earning higher incomes.

---

[3] They report that in 1994, 75% of single mothers, 67% of mothers separated from cohabitation and 51% of divorced mothers were unemployed/inactive.

[4] Similar income profiles appear in the analysis of Marsh, Ford and Finlayson (1997: Table 3.1).

Table 7.10: Main Source of Income of Mothers—Former Cohabiting and Formerly Married Parent Groups

(a) Former cohabiting parent group*
Main source of income of mothers

	Before separation n = 51 %	After separation n = 43 %	At interview n = 43 %
Social security b'ft	37	75	66
Mother's earnings	9	16	18
Father's earnings	37	–	–
Father's earnings plus social security	4	–	–
Maintenance	–	2	4
Both mother's and father's earnings	4	–	–
New partner's earnings	–	–	7
New partner and mother's earnings	–	–	2
Relatives	2	2	0
Unclear	6	0	0

(b) Formerly married parent group
Main source of income of mothers with children

	All mothers	Mothers looking after child	
	before separation n = 152 %	After separation n = 98[+] %	At interview n = 98[+] %
Social security b'ft	13	50	51
Mother's earnings	5	30	20
Mother's earnings plus social security	0	5	2
Father's earnings	67	–	–
Both own and father's earnings	16	–	–
New partner's earnings	–	5	18
New partner and mother's earnings	–	–	5
Maintenance	–	9	3
New partner and b'ft	–	1	0
New p'tner, b'ft and mother	–	–	1

* See Table 6.6(b).
[+] Information from women only; information unavailable in 2 cases.

Table 7.11: Income Levels over Time, Showing Fathers' Incomes—Formerly Married Parent Group

Income	All fathers	All fathers interviewed	
	before separation n = 133* Cum %	After separation n = 42[+] Cum %	At interview n = 48[++] Cum %
Under £4,000	5	2	4
£4,001 to £6,000	17	26	27
£6,001 to £8,000	31	36	33
£8,001 to £10,000	41	43	40
£10,001 to £12,000	49	55	46
£12,001 to £14,000	62	69	56
£14,001 to £16,000	75	86	77
Over £16,000	100	100	100

* Information unavailable in 19 cases.
[+] Information unavailable in 7 cases.
[++] Information unavailable in 1 case.

Table 7.12: Income Levels over Time, Fathers with Children Only—Formerly Married Parent Group

Income	Before separation n = 9 Cum %	After separation n = 7 Cum %	At interview n = 9 Cum %
Under £4,000	0	0	0
£4,001 to £6,000	11	14	22
£6,001 to £8,000	11	28	44
£8,001 to £10,000	22	43	44
£10,001 to £12,000	22	43	44
£12,001 to £14,000	33	57	56
£14,001 to £16,000	56	86	89
Over £16,000	100	100	100

Changes in family structures

After the separation, 142 out of 152 of the study children stayed with their mother. Ten (7 per cent) lived with the father, which is the same proportion of children who stayed with former cohabiting fathers (three out of fifty-one: 6 per cent). One study child was living with the father's parents. A full sibling of the study child was living with the other parent in three cases, the same number as in the former cohabiting parent group.

We have seen that, in the former cohabiting group, 35 per cent of the parents who were looking after the study child and 43 per cent of the "outside" parents had acquired a new partner (sometimes more than one) by the time of the interview. This was a higher incidence of subsequent partnering than in the "never-together" group (see Table 5.7). In the formerly married group, 40 per cent of the "caring" parents and 49 per cent of the "outside" parents had repartnered by the time of interview, which gave them the highest incidence of repartnering of all the groups. As with the other groups, the "outside" parents repartnered slightly more often than those living with the study child. It would seem that the older the parents are the more quickly do they form another relationship when that with the child's parent breaks down. Since we found that repartnering in the other groups seemed to have negative effects on contact with the child, this might seem to be an ominous finding for the children of formerly married parents.

CONTINUING PARENTING

Parenting during marriage

As in the case of the former cohabitants, we asked about the extent of shared parenting during the marriage. Many reported that this had occurred to some extent, but we required a strong indication of sharing before we classified the answer as demonstrating equal parenting. We found 27 out of 152 reports (17 per cent), compared to 12 per cent for the former cohabitants. However, there seemed to be a gender effect here because it was claimed by fifteen out of forty-nine (30 per cent) of the male respondents as against 11 out of 103 (11 per cent) of the women. But six claims by the fathers seemed well-founded because they were either looking after the study child or a sibling of the study child.

Contact and relationship between parents

The state of the relationship between the parents is shown in Table 7.13 which compares all the groups.

Marsh, Ford and Finlayson (1997: Table 2.4) also found that the formerly married had the best relationships, but did not show how these had changed over time. Our findings in this respect are unexpected, and very important. That the formerly married might have the worst relationships at the time of separation may have been anticipated on the intuition that the more that has been invested in a relationship, the more bitter its termination is likely to be. But we could not have predicted that, by the time of interview, 40 per cent of the formerly married parents claimed to have a fairly good or very good

Table 7.13: Relationships Between Parents—All Groups

	Good %	Neutral %	Bad %	No relationship %	Unknown %
At birth/separation					
Never-together (n=46)	28	11	17	39	4
Former cohabiting parent (n=51)	25	8	45	22	0
Formerly married parent (n=152)	24	14	50	12	0
At interview					
Never-together (n=46)	26	13	4	50	7
Former cohabiting parent (n=51)	24	27	14	35	0
Formerly married parent (n=152)	40	25	11	24	0

relationship with one another. This is in strong contrast to the other groups, where there was virtually no change in the proportion of good relationships over time, although there was a decline in bad ones. It is true that the "never-togethers" had fewer bad relationships at interview than the formerly married (4 per cent as against 11 per cent), but that was largely because so many had lost touch completely.

It does not seem that the sharing of parental responsibility for looking after the child has anything other than a slight influence on the subsequent state of the parents' relationships. The twenty-three "equal sharing" cases were distributed between the categories of relationship in very similar proportions as all the 152 cases in the "formerly married parent" group: namely, "good" (56 per cent), "neutral" (21 per cent), "bad" (17 per cent) and "no relationship" (4 per cent). They are slightly over-represented in the "good" category, but the numbers are small and we have already said that the category is to be viewed cautiously. What the cause of the improvement in relationships between the formerly married might be is considered later.

Contact between parents and children

Incidence and extent of contact
We now consider the evidence about the extent to which contact was retained between the "outside" parent and the study child. The cases divide into those where contact was maintained on a regular and committed basis (see pp. 70–1) from the time of separation ("continuing contact"), those where it was never

exercised ("no contact ever") and those where it either ceased or was so severely disrupted that it could not be said to continue in a substantial sense ("interrupted contact"). The comparisons with the other groups appear in Table 7.14.

Table 7.14: Contact Between "Outside" Parent and Child—All Groups

Contact	Never-together group n = 46 %	Former cohabiting parent n = 51 %	Formerly married group n = 152 %
Continuing contact	35	45	69
No contact ever	39	14	5
Interrupted/ended	15	23	27
Irregular	0	10	0
Restarted	0	6	0
False starts	13	0	0

It is plain that there is a much higher degree of contact in the case of the formerly married parents, despite the fact that the relationships between the parents at the time of the separation are the poorest (Table 7.13). Indeed, in 95 per cent of cases it was retained at that time, although in 27 per cent it was subsequently lost or severely disrupted. If we compare the position at the time of interview between the former cohabitants and the formerly married parents, 51 per cent of the former were in "committed" contact (including the three "restarts") and 69 per cent of the latter.[5]

When contact was exercised, the most common arrangements were for it to occur once (26 out of 105: 24 per cent) or twice (14 out of 105: 13 per cent) a week, without overnight stays. But overnight stays occurred in 26 out of 105 (25 per cent) of cases, at frequencies varying between once and four times a week. Some cases looked very close to equal parenting. Ten involved contact on four or more days a week, two of them including overnight stays. In such cases, especially where the child spends nights in each house, it is difficult to distinguish between the parent looking after the child and the "outside" parent. But we would estimate that this occurs in only somewhere between 2 and 10 per cent of cases of contact. At the other extreme, we included cases where contact involved overnight visits three times a year, or four nights every six months.

We asked whether the parents made joint decisions on important matters regarding the child's upbringing. Ten said that they did so, including one case where the father was looking after the child and another where the child was with the father's parents. But of the ten, only four said there was real equality on a day-to-day basis. The others confined it to episodic matters such as

---

[5] See Marsh, Ford and Finlayson (1997: Table 2.4) for a similar profile regarding contact.

healthcare, holiday plans and choice of schooling. This suggests that joint decision-making of any serious nature probably occurs only in about one in ten cases where contact is regularly exercised, and then usually only on a limited number of issues.

We now consider the various factors which may be associated with the exercise of contact.

Contact and distance between parent and child after separation

We have observed that in our earlier groups "outside" parents who were in contact with their children tended to live close by them, but also that many parents who lived nearby did not exercise contact. We could not say whether parents were exercising contact because they were living nearby, or whether they were living close to the child because they wished to continue contact. This was especially so as most had not repartnered.

When we look at the formerly married parents, we find that the tendency for "outside" parents to be living near the child has much diminished: Table 7.15.

Table 7.15: Proportion of "Outside" Parents in Contact Living within 10 miles of Child—All Groups

	Never-together group n = 16 %	Former cohabiting parent group n = 26* %	Formerly married group n = 105 %
% living with 10 miles	81	69	60

* Including 3 cases where contact restarted later.

So the formerly married who were in contact were almost evenly split between parents living within and more than ten miles from the child. Two were said to be living abroad. This carries the implication that distance need be no real barrier to the exercise of contact if that is desired, and that the large proportion of "outside" parents in the first two groups who are living more than ten miles from the child and are not exercising contact are not so much inhibited by distance from exercising contact as by other factors.

Ages of children at time of separation

The children in the "formerly married parents" group were not only older than the children in our other groups at the time of interview, but also at the time of the separation of the parents (Table 7.16).

78 per cent of the children of the former cohabiting parents had been under 5 when the separation between their parents took place. But only 42 per cent of the formerly married parents had broken up when the study child was under 5. One-third of this group had separated when the child was over 7,

Table 7.16: Ages of Children at Time of Separation— Former Cohabiting and Formerly Married Parents Groups

Ages	Former cohabiting parents n = 51 %	Formerly married parents n = 152 %
Under 2	45	12
2–4	33	30
5–6	8	20
7–10	12	23
Over 10	2	11

compared to only 14 per cent of the former cohabitants. It is plain that the children of married parents usually experienced a longer period of time living with both their parents than those of the former cohabitants. We will consider the possible effect of this on the maintenance of contact a little later (p. 132). One conclusion, however, which might be drawn from this evidence is that, when they do break down, unmarried cohabitations with children do so quicker than marital unions. The evidence does not establish this directly, partly because it is based only on relationships which produced a child, and partly because the age of the child can only be a proxy for the period of time the parties lived together. Indeed, it is plausible (see p. 19) that many couples might live together outside marriage and marry only when they decide to have a child. But that would mean that the cohabitations of married people are even longer than the age of their children would suggest. On the other hand, many unmarried cohabitants might live together for many years before having a child without marrying. We do not know the answers to these questions. We can, however, say that married people who later separate seem to live together longer *with the child* than unmarried people who later separate do.

Contact and relationships between parents
We have observed already that relationships between the formerly married were the worst of all groups at the time of separation, and therefore when contact would have started (p. 120). We also saw that these relationships improved quite dramatically over time. The improvements mostly occurred when contact was maintained. The extent to which this happened is set out in Table 7.17.

Thus, improvements in relationships between the formerly married parents were reported in 61 out of 105 (58 per cent) of cases where a parent maintained contact with the child, in 48 per cent of cases where a former cohabitant did this and in 31 per cent where an parent in the "never-together" group kept contact. In 28 out of 105 (27 per cent) of cases the relationship remained

Table 7.17: Improved Relationships Between Parents in Contact over Time—All Groups

	Never-together group	Former cohabiting parent group	Formerly married group
Total in contact	16	23	105
Improved rel'ship			
Very bad to fairly bad	0	0	3
Very bad to no rel'ship	0	0	5
Very bad to neutral	1	2	6
Very bad to fairly good	0	0	8
Very bad to very good	0	0	1
Bad to fairly good	0	0	1
Bad to very good	0	1	0
Fairly bad to neutral	1	3	7
Fairly bad to fairly good	0	1	9
Fairly bad to very good	0	0	4
No rel'ship to neutral	0	0	2
No rel'ship to fairly good	0	1	1
No rel'ship to very good	0	0	1
Neutral to fairly good	1	0	8
Neutral to very good	0	0	1
Good to very good	1	0	0
Fairly good to very good	1	3	4
Totals	5	11	61

unchanged. Ten of these were "fairly good" and five "very good". Two declined from "very good" to "fairly good". In total, therefore, at the time of interview 39 out of 105 (37 per cent) of the relationships between parents in contact were described as "fairly good" and 16 out of 105 (15 per cent) as "very good": thus 52 per cent were thought to be generally "good". Seven relationships (7 per cent) were described as "fairly bad", one as "bad" and one as "very bad". Two were described as "neutral" and five parents felt they had no relationship at all with the other parent.

The implications of these data are intriguing. Of course it can always be said that contact is unlikely to continue if relationships are poor, so that the continuation of contact is a reflection of the improving relationship between the parents. But contact tended to *begin* when the relationships were poor. Although there is evidence that the levels of conflict between parents do not necessarily affect the closeness of the relationship between the outside parent and the child,[6] our data at least open up the possibility that the exercise of

[6] Buchanan, Maccoby and Dornbusch (1996).

contact between a parent and the child operates in the long term to improve the relationships between the parents.

In the previous chapter, we noted that violence may have been present in at least 12 per cent of the former cohabiting parent cases (p. 94). This was mainly based on the occasions when personal protection was discussed with a lawyer. Among the formerly married, 23 out of 103 (22 per cent) of women, but no men, said that they had done this. One other case had involved kidnapping of the child by the father. It seems unlikely that a woman would discuss personal protection measures with a lawyer unless there was some real apprehension, and probable that there were other cases where the apprehension existed but the matter was not discussed with a lawyer. These figures do not provide a precise measure of the prevalence of violence, or its threat. Nor do they provide a basis for making comparisons between the various groups within our sample population. This is partly because they raise problems of interpretation of what constitutes violence and why the issue of personal protection was discussed, but also because the extent to which the possibility of violence was recorded by our data will be related to the extent to which members of the groups consulted a lawyer, thus providing a context in which the issue of personal protection might be raised. As will be seen, the formerly married were more likely than the other groups to consult a lawyer (p. 133).[7]

We can however observe that women who raised the issue of personal protection were more likely to have had a husband who was unemployed. The husband had been employed full-time before separation in 52 per cent of the cases where the issue arose (compared to 77 per cent employed full-time for the whole group) and 26 per cent were unemployed (compared to 16 per cent for the whole group). However, the men concerned were no more or less likely to continue to exercise contact with the child. Seventeen out of twenty-three (74 per cent) of them did this, compared to 69 per cent of the whole group. Concern has been expressed[8] about the continuation of contact between fathers and children where there is a background of violence, since the occasions where contact is exercised may be used to inflict further violence on the mother and the child (see p. 52). However, our data presents another side to this situation. Of the seventeen cases where contact continued on a regular basis despite the implication of violence, eight mothers reported that her relationship with the father improved from "very bad" or "fairly bad" to "fairly good" and one that it had become "very good". The proportion of "good" outcomes (nine out of seventeen: 53 per cent) is almost identical to those in the whole group where contact was maintained (52 per cent). In only three "violence" cases was the relationship described as "bad" at time of interview: one had remained "fairly bad"; another had moved from being "Non-existent" to "fairly bad" and the third had "improved" from being "very bad" to

---

[7] However, Marsh, Ford and Finlayson (1997: Table 2.1a) found evidence of violence in 35% of cases, but do not distribute these between the categories of lone parents.

[8] Hester and Radford (1996). See (1996) 26 *Family Law* 526.

"fairly bad". Four relationships were now "neutral" and one "non-existent". Our data therefore do not indicate that the presence of violence or its threat during the time the parties lived together *necessarily* imposes an obstacle to the general tendency for relationships between the parents to improve over time where the "outside" parent maintains contact with the child.[9]

Contact, employment and financial support
It appeared (p. 98) that for the former cohabitants there was no association between the father's employment status at the time of separation and the subsequent exercise of contact. This was also so for the formerly married parents. Excluding the fathers who were looking after the children, 68 per cent of all fathers retained "committed" contact, and this included 72 per cent of those in full-time employment. However there did seem to be a preponderance of unemployed fathers at time of interview among those whose contact had been seriously disrupted: 29 per cent of all cases (excluding the "custodial" fathers) experienced such disruption, but 47 per cent of the fathers who were unemployed at interview had done so. However, it seems unlikely that being unemployed was a reason for the failure of contact. This is because in the seven[10] cases where an unemployed father had lost contact, in five the child was under 2 at separation, in one the child was 2 and in the one case where the child was older (10), contact was in fact continuing, but on a two-monthly basis. We will see (p. 131) that children who are under 2 at separation are more likely to lose contact than keep it and the father's employment status may be irrelevant. However in eight cases the father had been unemployed at time of separation, and in five of them the child was under 2 at separation and in two the child was under 4. It may therefore be the case that the father's unemployment contributed to the early breakdown of these marriages and thus, indirectly, to the loss of contact with the child.

In looking at the payment of financial support, we find a discrepancy in reports between the men and women respondents, but it is a surprisingly small one. Excluding the cases involving custodial fathers, thirty-nine out of sixty-six (59 per cent) of women respondents in cases where the father was in committed contact with the child reported the receipt of financial support, and twenty out of thirty (63 per cent) of the men respondents said that they were paying. However, of the women who received the support, 11 per cent claimed that it was irregularly paid, whereas no man admitted to this. Similarly, where contact had been interrupted, fourteen out of twenty-five (56 per cent) of women claimed to receive support (two said it was irregular) and eight out of thirteen (61 per cent) of men said they were paying it.

If we combine the women and men respondents, and comparing all three groups, financial support is related to contact in the way set out in Table 7.18.

---

[9] Burgoyne and Clark (1984) show how violence can come to be regarded as a normal feature of daily life.

[10] We exclude here the case where the father was unemployed because he was in prison.

Table 7.18: Contact and Financial Support—All Groups

	Whether support paid				
	Regularly %	Irreg %	Not paid %	Unknown %	Number
Never-together group n = 46*					
Continuing contact	56	25	12	6	16
Interrupted contact	33	0	50	16	6
No contact ever	5	0	90	0	18
False starts	0	0	100	0	6
Former cohabiting parents n = 48**					
Contact continuing or restarted	24	8	68	0	25
Irregular contact	0	33	67	0	6
No contact or contact ended	12	18	71	0	17
Formerly married parents n = 141***					
Continuing contact	54	7	38	0	96
Interrupted contact	53	5	42	5	38
No contact ever	0	0	100	0	7

* Based on Table 5.6(b).
** Based on Table 6.14(a).
*** Excludes 11 cases where child was not with the mother.

If we compare the groups, we find that it is the formerly married fathers who are most likely to pay *something* (regularly or irregularly) to their former family. Ninety out of 141 (64 per cent) of all the formerly married mothers received some form of support. This proportion is remarkably close to the finding in our previous study (Eekelaar and Maclean (1986: 91)) where we found that "if we ... look only at those cases where a dependent child was still living with the mother at the time of the interview, and she had not remarried or begun cohabiting with another man, if we include mortgage payments, we find that income transfers were being made in 68 per cent of these cases". This compares to only 31 per cent of the former cohabiting parents who received some kind of support and 32 per cent of the "never-togethers".[11]

When we look a the payment of *regular* support, we find that this was paid in 82 out of 235 (35 per cent) of cases in our whole sample, which figure is close to the 30 per cent reported by Marsh, Ford and Finlayson (1997: Table 5.3). But our breakdown is different between the groups. The formerly married paid most frequently: 62 out of 141 (44 per cent), compared to twelve out of forty-six (26 per cent) for the "never-together" group and only eight out of forty-eight (16 per cent) for the former cohabitants. Marsh, Ford and Finlayson also found that 44 per cent of divorced mothers received regular

[11] Research by Jonathan Bradshaw, unpublished at the time this text went to press, found that 60 per cent of absent fathers were currently paying some maintenance: see Bennett (1997: 10).

maintenance, but that 14 per cent of single mothers and 26 per cent of former cohabiting mothers received it as well.

If we break our groups down according to the exercise of contact, we find that the best regular payers were those fathers in the "never-together" group who kept in continuing contact with the child (56 per cent) but we have suggested that this tends to continue for rather short periods. 54 per cent of the formerly married parents who exercised committed contact paid regularly. Where contact was never exercised, support was hardly ever paid in any of the groups. Although it is clear that fathers are not exercising contact *because* they are paying support, it is equally clear that there is a close link between the payment of financial support and the exercise of contact.

Our previous study was concerned primarily with spousal maintenance, which terminates when the recipient remarries. But the present study focused primarily on the children, and the child support obligation continues despite repartnering, and in fact whether the mother had repartnered made no difference to the payment of support. So 60 per cent of repartnered mothers in the formerly married group received regular payments from fathers who kept regular contact with the child, which compares well with the 54 per cent of all mothers who received regular payments from such men. Where contact was interrupted or ended, 56 per cent of repartnered mothers received regular support compared to 53 per cent of all the mothers. The repartnering of the mother was not therefore seen as being a ground for stopping support. (The figures for the "former cohabiting" parent group were too small to allow a comparison to be made with them on this issue).

Repartnering by the father is not a legitimate ground for failing to support the child. Where the father kept in contact, it seemed that his repartnering had no effect on his likelihood to pay: 58 per cent of repartnered fathers paid regularly (compared to 54 per cent of all fathers). But only 40 per cent of repartnered fathers who were *not* in contact paid regularly compared to 53 per cent of all fathers not in contact, so it seems that where contact is not exercised but payments are made, these will be threatened if the father repartners.

The overwhelming cause for not paying support is being out of work, either due to sickness, disability, unemployment or some other reason. 67 per cent of employed fathers, whether in contact or not, paid regular support, but only three of the thirty who were out of work paid anything. We wished to discover why a father who was in work might not pay.

In the case of those in contact, of the thirty-seven instances of non-payment, the following reasons appeared (Table 7.19).

If we look at the 28 cases where contact was interrupted, or never occurred, and no support was paid either, no plausible reason appeared in only three cases, though in five insufficient information was available. But in eight out of twenty-eight (28 per cent) the father was known to be unemployed, in four out of twenty-eight (14 per cent) he was known to be sick or disabled, in two he was in full-time education and in three he was in work, but had repart-

Table 7.19: Possible Reasons for Not Paying Support—Formerly Married Fathers

Possible reason	Number
Father sick/disabled	7
Father unemployed	9
Father employed (or status unknown)	
BUT	
(i) both repartnered	2
(ii) father repartnered	6
(iii) mother repartnered	2
Mother refused to accept payments	1
Clean break	1
Father about to start paying	1
Mother stayed in jointly owned home	5
Total possible reasons	34
Father reported to be in full-time work, no reason known	3
Total	37

nered. In one the mother had repartnered, in another the father was abroad and in another he was in prison.

If we add the cases together, we find that only a very small proportion (about 10 per cent) of formerly married fathers seem to be in full-time work, living on their own and paying *no* financial support for their children, rather fewer than in the case of the former cohabitants (14 per cent: see Table 6.15) and the "never-together" group (about 21 per cent: see p. 75). And even in these cases, the mothers may have repartnered, or may be living in the house which the father jointly owns. However we should express some caution about those fathers who had never been in contact with the child because our information about them was very limited.

Although many of the fathers were giving some form of financial support, the sums very often seemed to be very small. The reports by the women and men respondents were very similar. 90 per cent of women and 91 per cent of men reported sums of under £50 a week. In Table 7.20 we show the sums reported by sex of respondent. In this Table we have included sums which were ordered or agreed, or otherwise expected, but may not actually have been paid, or were paid infrequently.

So, in well over half the instances where money was expected to flow from one household to a child in another, the amount will be no more than £30 a week and only one in ten will be above £50 a week. This is consistent with the finding by Marsh, Ford and Finlayson (1997: Table 5.6) that the average amount of maintenance paid by lone parents who receive regular payments in 1994 was £39 a week, though it was rather higher for formerly married parents.

Table 7.20: Amounts of Financial Support Paid—Formerly Married Parent Group: Men and Women Respondents

Weekly sums	Men reporting n = 35 Cum %	Women reporting n = 62 Cum %
Up to £10	17	21
Up to £30	77	68
Up to £50	91	90
Up to £70	91	98
Up to £100	94	98
Up to £120	100	100

The Child Support Agency had been in touch with forty-three out of ninety-eight of the fathers who were in contact with the study child; in three cases where the father was looking after the child, the Agency had been in contact with the mother. In five cases orders had been made. It had also approached twelve out of thirty-nine of the fathers whose contact was interrupted (with three orders) and one of the seven who had never been in contact.

Contact and repartnering

In Chapters 5 and 6 we saw that the exercise of contact seemed to be most strongly influenced by whether either or both of he parents was living with someone other than the other parent. For the "never-together" group, remaining "unpartnered" came close to being a condition necessary for the continuation of contact. For the formerly cohabiting group, the age of the child at separation was significant, but the continued contact with older children tended to be also accompanied by an absence of repartnering. We had an insufficient number of cases to be sure whether the absence of repartnering or the age of the child were more important. In the case of the formerly married we can see that it is the age of the child which seems to be determinative (Table 7.21).

Table 7.21 shows that where a child is under 2 at time of separation, contact was less likely to be maintained than to be maintained. Only eight out of twenty-six (31 per cent) kept contact, whereas for the over-2s contact was retained in 96 out of 126 (76 per cent) of cases. We saw (p. 100) that there was a similar pattern for those who had not married, where 35 per cent of children under 2 at separation kept contact compared to 54 per cent of children who were over 2. However, we also saw that, for the children of the former cohabitants, it may have been important that neither of their parents had repartnered, although this could not be stated with certainty. But in the case of the formerly married, the possibility that repartnering was a stronger influence than the age of the child at separation seems unlikely. In their case,

Table 7.21: Contact and Repartnering—Formerly Married Parent Group

	Contact continuing	Contact interrupted	No contact ever	Totals
Children under 2				
"Outside" parent only r'ptd	3	1	0	4
"Caring" parent only r'ptd	1	2	0	3
Both parents r'ptd	0	7	0	7
Neither parent r'ptd	4	8*	0	12
Not known	0	0	0	0
Sub-total	8	18	0	26
Children 2–4				
"Outside" parent only r'ptd	5*	3	1	9
"Caring" parent only r'ptd	6	2	1	9
Both parents r'ptd	9	3	1	13
Neither parent r'ptd	11*	2	0	13
Not known	0	0	1	1
Sub-total	31	9	4	44
Children 5–6				
"Outside" parent only r'ptd	8*	2	0	10
"Caring" parent only r'ptd	5*	0	0	5
Both parents r'ptd	5	2	0	7
Neither parent r'ptd	7	0	0	7
Not known	0	1*	0	1
Sub-total	25	5	0	30
Children 7–10				
"Outside" parent only r'ptd	9*	1	0	10
"Caring" parent only r'ptd	4*	0	0	4
Both parents r'ptd	5	1	0	6
Neither parent r'ptd	11*	2	2	15
Not known	0	0	0	0
Sub-total	29	4	2	35
Children over 10				
"Outside" parent only r'ptd	4	1	1	6
"Caring" parent only r'ptd	2	1	0	3
Both parents r'ptd	2	2	0	4
Neither parent r'ptd	3	0	1	4
Not known	0	0	0	0
Sub-total	11	4	2	17
Totals	104	40	8	152

* Includes one father with care.

while eight out of twenty-six (31 per cent) of all children under 2 at separation kept contact, 33 per cent (four out of twelve) of those whose parents had not repartnered retained contact, suggesting this factor was of no special importance. For those over 2, where contact was likely to continue (96 out of 126: 76 per cent), it was retained in thirty-two out of thirty-nine (82 per cent) of cases where the parents had not repartnered; in twenty-six out of thirty-five (74 per cent) where the outside parent only repartnered; in nineteen out of twenty-one (90 per cent) of cases where the caring parent only repartnered and twenty-one out of thirty (70 per cent) of cases where both had repartnered. While there was slightly less contact when both repartnered, it seemed to make little difference if one or the other had done so. The time between separation and interview did not affect the matter.[12]

We should, perhaps, be cautious in comparing the effects of repartnering with the "former cohabiting parent" group, where numbers were small. It would seem, however, that the age of the child at separation is a very significant factor and that this is at least one explanation for the higher contact between formerly married parents and their children. The sequence may run thus: formerly married people are likely to have lived together with the child for longer than the unmarried cohabitants; the child is more likely to be older at separation; therefore contact is more likely to continue for the formerly married. In the case of the formerly married we can also add: where contact has become relatively established (for the above reasons), repartnering is less likely to disturb its continuation. It is not clear whether this last statement can be made in the case of the former cohabitants. On our present data, it cannot.

Table 7.22: Length of Time Between Separation and Interview by Age of Child at Separation

Age of child	Under 2	2–4	5–6	7–9	Over 10
Under 2 (n = 24) Cum %	17	46	62	83	100
Over 2 (n = 128) Cum %	19	54	74	89	100
All (n = 152)	18	53	72	88	100

CONCLUSIONS

In conclusion, the evidence seemed to indicate that marriages represented a higher degree of investment in the parental relationship than was the case for the "never-togethers" and the former cohabitants. At the material level, this appeared in the greater economic prosperity of the married couples compared

---

[12] For a statistical note, see Methodological Appendix.

to the other groups. At the relationship level, the longer periods which married parents lived together before separating seemed to suggest a greater commitment to the relationship than was present in the case of the cohabitants. We emphasize that we are not arguing that marriage *causes* higher stability and commitment. Our data cannot tell us whether it does or does not. What does certainly appear to be the case, however, is that people who *already enjoy* a reasonably high level of stability in their economic and social circumstances, and perhaps also in their personal relationship, tend to locate their role as parents within the framework of marriage. Marriage is an outward sign of stable, joint parenthood. For the study children, of course, this meant that the social capital for the children of married parents was all the more substantial.

But all our cases were of marriages that had already proved unstable. We have observed, however, that in many of these the economic foundations of the partnership had become undermined by unemployment before the separation. This is consistent with evidence that the less economically secure unions are at greater risk of collapse. But because these were *marriages* their unravelling was more complex than was the process by which the parents in the other groups faced their future. 53 per cent of married parents saw a lawyer and no other professional; a further 20 per cent saw a lawyer *and* another professional.[13] Only 19 per cent sought no professional advice at all. But 60 per cent of the former cohabitants took no professional advice, and only 22 per cent went to a lawyer. Similarly, only two "never-together" mothers consulted a lawyer. We should add that 79 per cent of the parents who saw a lawyer were legally aided.

Seeing a lawyer does not necessarily mean that the issue will come to court. We found only one case where matters concerning the children (in this case, residence) needed resolution by a court. We found no case where an "outside" parent needed to have recourse to a court to enforce contact. On the contrary, there were two cases where a mother asked a lawyer whether the father could be compelled to exercise it! As far as financial support was concerned, in one-third of the fifty-six cases where it was paid regularly when the parents were in contact, this was being regulated by a court (nineteen cases). The rest were voluntary payments under some informal arrangement. There were seven other court orders, but these were either being complied with irregularly or not at all. We do not, of course, know whether the payments made under court orders would not have been made at all were it not for the order. However, this seems unlikely. Where contact was not being exercised at all, or only infrequently, we noted that financial support was also rarely paid (Table 7.18). In the relatively few cases where it was paid regularly in those circumstances (14/53 cases: 26 per cent), only two payments were made under court orders. Court orders existed in two other cases, but were not followed.

---

[13] 3/152 saw a mediator; 14 saw a counsellor from Relate; 13 consulted a doctor or priest.

Hence it seems that court orders played a very small role in the payment or non-payment of financial support. The exercise of contact was far more important. Nor were the payments made by court orders any higher than those made without a court order, but we can say little about levels of support in the absence of more detailed information about relative incomes.

One might explain these disparities between the groups with regard to professional and institutional involvement on the grounds that, being a legal framework, marriage demands legal advice when it runs into difficulties. This is probably only partly true. Respondents were asked what they consulted lawyers about. They almost always said it was about custody, money or property, often all three, and (as we saw: p. 125) sometimes domestic violence. These substantial matters seemed to arise much more frequently when married parents separated than in the case of the other groups. It is also true, however, that relationships were maintained between the child and both parents after the separation more commonly when the parents had been married (and payment of support was also more frequent) even though these parents often repartnered. It might therefore be suggested that the initiation of cross-household parenthood, especially in circumstances where a relationship lasting some years has broken down, can be a complex matter which frequently requires some kind of external advice. This does not imply that the matter needs to be resolved by a court, and we saw that when financial support was paid this was done under court order in less than one-third of cases. But some kind of external advice, guidance or regulation seems important. If we put it another way: we have no reason to believe that, had the former cohabiting parents lived together as long as the formerly married parents in the same social conditions and maintained the same levels of post-separation contact with the children, they would not also have resorted to professional (particularly legal) help to the same extent as the formerly married.

8

The Parental Obligation and Cross-Household Parenthood

We stated in Chapter 1 that the central concern of this study was to consider how far parenthood in itself acted as a mediating mechanism for the creation of legal and social obligations (p. 1). We explained that, while we can describe legal rules, we could not directly prove the existence of social rules. However, we claimed that our data could indicate from people's behaviour and from evidence of their attitudes when the presence of social obligations might be *assumed* (p. 7). This chapter therefore begins by summarizing the main empirical findings of the research. It then gives the results of the survey of our respondents' attitudes. The chapter concludes by considering, first, how this information bears on some issues of current concern to family law policy and then, how far it allows us to construct assumptions about the social and legal obligations operating on parents when they are not living together with their children. In making our conclusions about those obligations we take a further step and also offer some evaluations of our own, sometimes asking and answering the questions: what should these obligations be? Should certain obligations be encouraged or discouraged?

SUMMARY OF MAIN FINDINGS

A. Cross-household parenting arises from a variety of distinctive familial experiences; three main groupings can be distinguished

1. Concern about the social capital available to children who do not live with both of their natural parents should not be confined to children whose parents have divorced because the parents of over one-third of those children had not married each other. This third is roughly evenly divided between those who had lived together with the child but outside marriage (former cohabiting parents) and those who had never lived with the child at the same time ("never-together" group) (p. 60).

2. The familial relationships of children both of whose parents had never lived together with them can be very diverse. Sometimes the parents had lived together before the child was born; sometimes the fathers were in existing relationships and never commenced any kind of relationship with the children;

sometimes fathers, although living apart, became fathers of later siblings of the child. But these are numerically very small sub-groups (pp. 63–4).

3. The mothers in the "never-together" group were younger than the formerly cohabiting mothers, who, in turn, were younger than the formerly married mothers. The ages of the children reflected this (p. 108).

B. Findings mainly related to the "never-together" group

4. The mothers in the "never-together" group were financially the worst off when the child was born, 87 per cent of those living in independent households having incomes below £6,000 (p. 65), but 46 per cent of the mothers were living with their own parents. Most of these, however, moved out, usually when the child was in its second year, almost always into the rented sector (p. 66)

5. It took longer for the children whose parents had never lived together to acquire a stepfather than children in the other groups (p. 119). Only six out of twenty-three (26 per cent) of those who were over 5 at interview had a stepfather. We did not know, however, how often the parents of children born to parents who are living apart may later live together with each other (pp. 62–3).

6. In the "never-together" group, the fathers most likely to be in contact were those living with their own parents, and those least likely to be in contact were those in existing relationships. But where the fathers were living with their own parents, the children were younger. The presence of a partner of either parent seemed to be an important factor associated with lack of parental contact in the "never-together" group (p. 77). Financial support was hardly ever paid for children in that group where contact was not maintained, but was paid where contact was sustained (Table 7.18). In general, contact and support was offered on a fairly regular basis to about one-third of the children in that group, especially by fathers still living with their own parents, but this did not seem often to survive the father's departure from home especially if he or the mother acquired a partner. However, the relationships between the parents were the least conflictual in the whole sample, though they were also more likely to be "non-existent" (Table 7.17).

C. Findings mainly related to the "former cohabiting parent" group

7. The findings are consistent with other evidence that cohabiting parents have a less successful socio-economic profile than married parents, but also suggest that, like married couples, the less successful unmarried cohabitants are more vulnerable to instability than those cohabitants who enjoy better socio-economic conditions (p. 88).

8. The evidence shows that where unmarried parents separate, they are likely to do so when their children are younger than when married parents separate, indicating that unmarried cohabitations which produce children and which terminate do so more quickly than married cohabitations. The evidence also suggests that unmarried cohabitations which produce children may break up more frequently than married cohabitations which produce children (p. 88).

9. There was evidence that formerly cohabiting parents in owner-occupation enter into similar kinds of arrangements concerning the occupation of the home after separation as divorcing parents do.

D. Findings related particularly to post-separation contact between parent and child and joint decision-making between parents

10. Contact between the outside parent and the child was maintained most frequently by formerly married parents (69 per cent); next by former cohabiting parents (45 per cent) and then by fathers in the "never-together" group (35 per cent) (Table 7.14).

11. When contact was exercised, the most common arrangements were for it to occur once or twice a week, without overnight stays. But overnight stays occurred in 25 per cent of cases where contact was exercised by a formerly married father, at frequencies varying between once and four times a week, and some cases looked very close to equal parenting (p. 121).

12. There was little evidence of widespread "joint" parenting or joint decision-making either while the parents were living together or afterwards in any of our groups. There were no reports of this at all in the "never-together" group. There were indications that joint parenting during cohabitation might be slightly more common among the formerly married than the former cohabitants (17 per cent against 12 per cent) (p. 119), but none of the former cohabitants reported joint decision-making after the separation, whereas 10 per cent of the formerly married parents who remained in contact reported this on some issues (p. 122).

13. The evidence indicated that the distance an "outside" parent lived from the child was not a significant factor in the exercise of contact where that was desired (p. 122).

14. Repartnering by either parent was most common among the formerly married (p. 119). However, in the case of the formerly married, this did not affect the exercise of contact with the child or the payment of support. The most important factor associated with the continuation of contact was the age of the child at separation; the older the child, the more likely contact was to continue and support to be paid. In the case of the former cohabitants, it was not clear whether the age of the child at separation or repartnering were more important in the continuation of contact.

15. The reason why contact was most likely to continue in the case of the formerly married parents seems to have been that the children of the formerly married parents were older when the parents separated than was the case for the former cohabitants (p. 132).

E. Relationships between parents after separation

16. The relationships between the formerly married parents on separation were the worst relationships in the entire sample. In addition, there was evidence that at least 22 per cent of the mothers in this group may have experienced violence because they had discussed the issue of personal protection with a lawyer. There was also evidence of possible violence in 12 per cent of the former cohabitants' cases, but none for the "never-together" group. But a comparison of the possible incidence of violence between the groups cannot be made because the main indicator was the discussion of personal protection with a lawyer, and there was differential recourse to lawyers between the groups (p. 125).

17. In all groups, the continuation of contact with the child was associated with an improvement in the relationships between the parents. This was most noticeable in the case of the formerly married parents, despite the higher incidence of initially poor relationships between them. Contact was just as likely to continue in cases where personal protection had been discussed and the parties' relationships improved in the same way in those cases as in those where there was no evidence of violence (p. 124).

F. Findings related to employment, income patterns and housing

18. There was little difference in the employment patterns of formerly married and formerly cohabiting mothers in the period before the separation. Nor did these patterns differ from those of actually married and cohabiting mothers. The difference in the socio-economic status between the formerly cohabiting and formerly married groups, and between those groups and actually married and cohabiting parents, was related to the employment patterns of the fathers, not the mothers (p. 110).

19. Employment of the mothers in the "never-together" group increased slightly after the child's birth (from 7 per cent to 18 per cent). But for the former cohabitants and formerly married mothers who were looking after children, separation led to lower employment. But where they had not repartnered, these groups of mothers were more likely to be employed than those in the "never-together" group (former cohabitants: 30 per cent; formerly married: 39 per cent) (p. 114).

20. The employment of the formerly cohabiting mothers had dropped sharply after the separation, whereas that of the formerly married remained

much the same. The difference was largely a result of the fact that many fewer former cohabitants worked part-time (Table 7.8).

21. Both the formerly cohabiting and formerly married mothers suffered severe income-drops on separation; 75 per cent of the former and 50 per cent of the latter reported social security as their main income source (Table 7.10). The former cohabitants had nearly recovered to their pre-separation levels by the time of interview, whereas the formerly married fell far short of that, their income profiles now very closely matching those of the former cohabitants. However, they had started from higher levels than the former cohabitants (Table 7.9).

22. The formerly married fathers also suffered income drops at separation, but recovered fully by the time of interview, unless they were looking after children, when their position was only slightly better than that of the formerly married mothers (p. 116).

23. Financial support was hardly ever paid in any of the groups where contact was not exercised. For the "never-together" and "former cohabiting parent" groups its regular payment was almost entirely confined to cases where contact was continuing. For the married parents, it was as likely to be paid whether contact was regular or interrupted. But generally formerly married mothers were much more likely to receive some form of support from the father (64 per cent) than the others (31 per cent for former cohabitants and 32 per cent for the "never-together" group) (p. 127). Only 10 per cent of formerly married fathers were known to be in full-time work, living on their own and paying no financial support; the proportion was much higher for former cohabitants (29 per cent) and in the never-together group (30 per cent). Unlike the other groups, formerly married fathers who remained in contact continued to pay support whether or not they had repartnered (p. 128).

24. There appears to have been an increase over the last decade in the proportion of cases where formerly married women stay in the matrimonial home after separation. Fathers tended to decline further in housing status after separation than mothers (pp. 112–3).

G. Findings related to legal process

25. The suggestion made at the opening of the book (p. 2) that the law may be legally more implicated when family members live apart than when they live together was not directly addressed, since we did not consider cases where parents remained together. However, the findings suggested that any such proposition would require some refinement. There was an increasing degree of external involvement, from the minimal in the case of the parents who had never lived together with the child, to higher involvement in the case of the former cohabitants, and the greatest involvement for the formerly married (p. 133). The high degree of legal intervention in the case of the

formerly married may be explained by the requirement of a legal process for the dissolution of the marriage, so that parents were likely to use the necessity of a legal encounter to raise issues which went beyond the mere dissolution process into, for example, matters concerning the property or the children. However, it is also possible that the extent to which external intervention was sought was related to the length of time which the parents had lived together as parents before separating and to the corresponding extent to which they sought to sustain aspects of their parenthood after separation. If that is the case, the evidence suggests that parents find it difficult to maintain continuity of their parenthood after separation by their unaided efforts, thus supporting the suggestion that law tends to be more implicated in family relationships when people live apart than when they live in the same household *at least when those relationships are an extension of family relationships which had been previously exercised within a household to a significant degree.*

THE ATTITUDINAL SURVEY

Respondents' attitudes were elicited by presenting all of them with three scenarios. In this way we could gauge varied responses to a standard stimulus which was relevant to their own experiences. This was done in the following manner. Respondents were shown a card which stated:

" 1. Take a married couple, who have two young children. The marriage breaks down, and the man later starts a relationship with a new partner who already has two children of her own.
(a) As far as financial support is concerned, who do you think should come highest in the man's priorities—his *own* biological children who are living apart from him, or the children of his new partner?
(b) Should the fact that the man is now living with a second family affect the amount of financial support he gives to his first family?

2. Now imagine that the man has another child of his own with his new partner. Should this affect the financial support he is giving to his first family?

3. Now imagine that the man's *first* wife remarries. What do you think should happen now to the maintenance arrangements?"

It will be noted that the scenarios all presupposed the more "traditional" case of birth within marriage. At the end of an already long interview we wished to avoid cases which depended too much on individual circumstances which would encourage too many responses of the "it depends" kind. We therefore chose to focus on the standard case of parenthood within marriage, but in a way which raised the central concerns of this study: the conflict of the responsibilities of parenthood when a parent has a child in another household.

Analysis showed that the most significant variations in response were gender related. The answers to the questions were as shown in Table 8.1.

Table 8.1: Answers to Attitudinal Survey

Question 1 (a): priority between own children and stepchildren

	own %	stepchildren %	equal %	depends %
Fathers (n = 61)	59	8	22	11
Mothers (n = 188)	73	9	10	8
Total (n = 249)	70	7	14	9

Question 1 (b): should stepchildren affect financial support of first family?

	yes %	no %	depends %
Fathers (n = 61)	66	18	16
Mothers (n = 188) parents	37	46	17
Total (n = 249)	44	39	17

Question 2: should subsequent own child affect the support to the first family?

	yes %	no %	depends %
Fathers (n = 61)	42	40	18
Mothers (n = 188)	28	58	14
Total (n = 249)	31	54	15

Question 3: what should happen if the first wife remarries?

	No change %	Payments reduced %	Stop paying for wife %	Stop paying for child %	Depends/ other %
Fathers (n = 61)	26	11	7	29	27
Mothers (n = 188)	45	11	12	11	21
Total (n = 249)	40	11	11	16	22

The results show a strong attachment of mothers to a support obligation founded on natural parenthood, whereas the fathers relate the obligation much more closely to social parenthood. To the opening, general, question of priority between the man's natural children and his stepchildren, the majority of both fathers and mothers (but more mothers) thought the man's own children should come highest in his priorities. However, without necessarily changing this order of priority, 66 per cent of men felt that the fact that a father is living with stepchildren should *affect* the amount he gives his first family, whereas only a minority of the mothers felt the same. The mothers, in other words, held to their sense of priority without making allowances for the father's stepfamily. Also, despite their attachment to the father's obligation to his natural children, most mothers were unwilling to alter this priority even in favour of a later *natural* child of the father. The fathers, however, were equally divided as to whether a new child of his own should make any difference. About half of them, it seems, made no distinction between their own child and stepchildren in the father's new social family.

The men were also equally divided as to whether the father should continue to pay for his children if the mother remarried, but, consistently with their favouring of the social family, were more likely than the mothers to think that he should stop paying, transferring the burden to the new social father. The mothers, equally consistently, were much more likely to think that the remarriage should make no difference, though only 45 per cent expressed this view positively. Others were prepared to accept reduced payments or less for the mother only.

We should compare the results of our attitudinal survey to the relevant findings of a large Australian study which asked respondents for their views about various aspects of parental responsibility (Funder and Smyth, 1996). This found that 91 per cent of Australians thought that parents should "share" financial support of their children after divorce or separation and 87 per cent thought they should do this if they had lived together without being married. However, if the parents had never lived together, the percentage thinking that financial support should be shared dropped to 76 (Funder and Smyth (1996: 28)). Divorced parents gave similar answers to the general population. It is possible that similar results might be found in the United Kingdom, and, if so, that would demonstrate a very widespread ethic that in principle the costs of parenthood should be shared between the parents irrespective of their marital status. However, our data demonstrate that the readiness of fathers to act on this ethic is strongly influenced by a combination of the social relationship they enjoyed with the child and any subsequent social relationships they may develop with other children. Our attitudinal data reveals that fathers adjust the extent of the obligation which they feel they owe towards their natural children by reference to their subsequent social parenthood whereas mothers do not think they should do this.

SOME POLICY ISSUES

The comparison between our three groups threw into sharp relief the very distinctive character of parenthood which is undertaken within marriage. The extent of continuing, committed, contact (69 per cent) and its resilience to subsequent repartnering suggested that parenthood continues to be exercised in some form by the "outside" parent in over two-thirds of cases where marriages break down. This is supplemented by a similar incidence of provision of financial assistance of some kind (64 per cent), which is frequently associated with the exercise of contact. The contrast with former cohabiting parents is stark. Only 45 per cent maintained contact; financial assistance was even lower (31 per cent). Even this degree of continued parenting seemed vulnerable to subsequent repartnering.

An immediate policy implication might seem to be that marriage is in itself a more propitious context in which to rear children than out-of-wedlock unions. This is to make the assumption, of course, that contact with the "outside" parent is desirable from the child's point of view. We will return to this later (p. 147), but accepting the assumption at this point, one must still be cautious about drawing such a conclusion. This is because there can be little doubt that parents who are married have a different socio-economic profile than those who are not. Our evidence shows two respects in which they differ from other parents when they are together: they enjoy a higher degree of material wealth and security and, if they eventually do part, they will have lived together with the child for longer. We cannot conclude that it is marriage which creates the higher degree of material wealth and security of married people, for it may be that people are inclined to marry only when they have such wealth and security. The particular vulnerability to divorce of less materially successful married people suggests that these social factors sustain marriage rather than the other way around. The greater the length of time which married parents live together before separating (if they do separate) may also be a function of their relatively more successful circumstances.

If this analysis is correct, we should identify the socio-economic status of the parents rather than their formal relationship as having the most significant effect on the social capital which they provide for their children. However, marriage may play an important role in symbolizing and confirming an achieved degree of economic security, and therefore be a desirable context in which parenthood is to be exercised. We cannot determine from this study how much *being married* might *in itself* add to the security created by socio-economic circumstances, or whether other types of institutional arrangements (for example, making parental responsibility agreements) might have similar effects. We can see value in institutionalizing the expectations inherent in the joint exercise of parenthood and note that, insofar as this is done through marriage, most people make the public commitment which marriage symbolizes when their socio-economic circumstances are such that their chances of providing the most favourable social capital for their children are at their highest. For this reason, whatever might be the position regarding childless marriages, our evidence reveals marriage in a positive light as an institution which supports parenthood.

In the context of present policy concerns, these reflections lead us to question whether the degree of concern over "saving" marriages which was demonstrated at a political level during the passage of the Family Law Bill 1996 might have been misplaced. This is not to deny the obvious point that happily married parents are more likely to create a better environment for childrearing than unhappily separated parents. Also, our findings reinforce many others in demonstrating the decline in material resources after divorce of women with children. But, despite the disturbances which divorce clearly bring (and we noticed the extent to which inter-spousal relationships deteriorated at the time of separation), the continued exercise of parenthood showed a surprising resilience, and through its exercise, the relationships between the parents themselves frequently improved. The Family Law Act's construction of a panoply of mechanisms (information meetings, counselling, mediation) to deter divorce or to "improve" the quality of its outcome may be an excessive reaction.

On the other hand, legislation and policy hitherto has paid scant attention to the parenthood of unmarried cohabitants. Although, as described in Chapter 3, unmarried parents have now been given more legal recognition, and with it, wider legal remedies, the position of children of broken unmarried cohabitations is entirely neglected in comparison to the attention given to the children of divorced parents. Yet our findings show that their position is likely to be much more precarious than the latter. The relationships between their parents seemed less secure than those between married parents and, although the socio-economic circumstances of formerly married mothers in the longer term was not very different from that of the former cohabiting mothers, the children of former cohabitants were less likely to sustain a relationship with their father. Consequently, these children were less likely to receive financial support from the "outside" parent. This evidence suggests that the approach reflected in some aspects of the Family Law Act 1996 that, in order to enhance the status of marriage, the legal protection given to unmarried cohabitants and former cohabitants should be explicitly inferior to that offered to married people[1] is very misguided as far as it covers unmarried cohabitants with children and supports any measures which may be proposed[2] to enhance legal remedies available to benefit them. We have suggested, though, that their greater vulnerability may be a function of the socio-economic circumstances rather than the lack of marital status of their parents. From the child's point of view, therefore, a couple should, if possible, commence their *joint parenthood* when they have attained a reasonable degree of social and financial stability. It is likely (though not inevitable) that they would then do this within the framework of marriage.

---

[1] This is apparent in the following provisions concerning protection against violence: (i) where the parties are married the courts are bound to make an occupation order where a child is likely to suffer significant harm if an order is not made unless the respondent is likely to suffer as greater or greater harm. Where, however, an applicant is a cohabitant or former cohabitant without any interest in the property, no such duty arises in those circumstances and occupation orders are limited to twelve months whereas there is no limit for married or formerly married people; (ii) in the case of cohabitants and former cohabitants, the courts must "have regard to the fact that they have not given each other the commitment involved in marriage": Family Law Act 1996, ss. 33 (7), (10), 35(8), (10), 36(8), (10), 41(2).

[2] For example, by the Law Commission in its examination of the position of homesharers.

The Family Law Act 1996 gives rise to a further ground for concern in the long waiting periods laid down by the Act from the initiation of the process through an information meeting to the earliest date for the granting of the divorce. This is twelve months or, if there are children or if one party insists, eighteen months, and can never be earlier than 21 months, or if there are children or one party insists, two years and three months, from the wedding.[3] The longer these periods, the greater the chance that one or both of the parties will enter into an unmarried cohabitation and produce a child while they are waiting for the divorce to come through. Our evidence about post-marital cohabitants lacked strength because of the small number in our sample, but there was nothing to suggest that their position was very different from all the cohabitants. It might therefore seem unfortunate to create circumstances which could encourage an increase in this class.

The Family Law Act 1996 also builds into the divorce process a strong bias towards the use of mediation rather than legal representation by applicants who seek legal aid. Before publicly funded legal representation can be granted, the Act requires the applicant to attend a meeting with a mediator, and the *mediator* must decide whether mediation is "suitable to the dispute" and "whether mediation could take place without either party being influenced by fear of violence or other harm". If the mediator decides in favour of mediation but the applicant prefers legal representation, the mediator's decision must be taken into account by the Legal Aid Board in deciding whether to grant aid for legal representation.[4] It seems likely that funding for legal representation will be denied in many cases. Our findings that half of formerly married mothers with children and three-quarters of formerly cohabiting mothers with children were primarily dependent on social security payments at the time of their separation indicates that a very large proportion of separating mothers will fall within this provision should it be brought into effect. We also saw that the separation affected the fathers' incomes hardly at all. This is of particular concern because a father can effectively deprive the mother of access to legal representation simply by deciding to participate in mediation even though he retains legal representation for himself from his own resources.

We were also struck by the degree of involvement which many fathers who had never lived together with the mother and the child had in at least the early years of the child's life. We do not know to what extent such fathers might later live with the mother of the child, nor to what extent the wider families of the mothers and the fathers become involved in the child's upbringing. It seemed possible that these wider kin networks might provide a basis for support for the continuation of a parental role by the father which might not exist in the case of former cohabiting fathers (whether married or unmarried) who

---

[3] Family Law Act 1996, ss. 7(3), (6), (13), 8(2).
[4] Family Law Act 1996, s. 29.

had lived with the mother and child for only a short time. This was a matter on which we felt further research might profitably be undertaken.

It does seem clear from our evidence, however, that the rule that an unmarried father does not acquire "parental responsibility" unless either granted by a court or acquired by agreement with the mother recorded in court (see p. 35) should be reconsidered. As we argued earlier (p. 49), the English concept of "parental responsibility" does not confer on its holder any better rights vis-à-vis the child than the other parent. Nor, we should add (unlike the position in Scotland: see p. 148), does it seem to confer enforceable rights on the child. Rather, it legitimates the actual exercise of parenthood by a natural parent and, where specifically provided, by a social parent. We noticed that the relationships between the "never-together" fathers and the mothers were characterized by extreme informality. We have no evidence that any of those who kept contact with the child took steps to formalize their relationship through a "parental responsibility" agreement or order. An average of about 4,300 "parental responsibility" agreements were recorded and about 4,000 orders made each year from 1992 to 1995.[5] Since in 1994 alone 216,000 babies were born outside marriage (see p. 20) it is clear that "parental responsibility" is acquired by only a tiny proportion of unmarried fathers. Yet, as we have seen, apart from the 55 per cent of fathers who are probably living with the mother (see p. 20), a significant minority who are not living with her are involved with the child, at least initially. Although, as we saw earlier (p. 137), not having "parental responsibility" probably seldom makes much *practical* difference in most cases, there can be some disadvantages, and the involvement of cohabiting, formerly cohabiting and "never-together" fathers with their children should surely be given legal recognition.

OBLIGATIONS

We conclude our study by returning to the issues put forward at the beginning of the book concerning the nature of the parental obligation.

Marital or parental obligations?

In Chapter 1 we referred to Irene Théry's thesis on *démariage*, and Chapter 3 described the way the legal developments have diminished the role of marriage as an institutional source of legal obligations, while increasing the significance of parenthood in this respect. Yet our findings have shown that, in England and Wales at any rate, the framework of marriage is associated

---

[5] Lowe (1997). Lowe believes a strong argument can be made that *all* fathers should be ascribed parental responsibility. This might be required by the European Convention on Human Rights.

with the establishment of a joint parental relationship which frequently continues beyond the termination of the marriage. Does this mean that parental obligations should be grounded in the institution of marriage?

Our earlier observations on the socio-economic context of marriage demonstrate that it is important not to confuse the formal institution with its substance, for to do so risks creating the illusion that the institution generates the social context with which it is associated. While marriage may therefore be a desirable context for parenthood in its reflection of and association with resources and stability and might properly be encouraged, policy should not attempt to develop a social *obligation* that parenthood must always be undertaken in marriage by, for example, imposing penalties upon parenthood which is undertaken outside marriage. This suggests that any obligations of parenthood should not be related to institutional formality but to the fact of parenthood.

Cross-household parenthood

We remarked above that our observation that marriage appeared to be a more successful context for the initiation of joint parenthood than unmarried cohabitation was premised on somewhat narrow assumptions about what the conditions for successful parenthood might be. We have confined ourselves to relating these to the concept of social capital discussed earlier (p. 48). We have drawn attention in Chapter 4 to the state of the evidence concerning the effect of family disruption, and in particular of events subsequent to such disruption, on various measures of children's well-being. There it was seen that it was by no means clear that the continuation of contact between children and an "outside" parent necessarily enhanced their "well-being", assessed by various criteria such as emotional and behavioural adjustment, though it could provide access to social capital which would not have been available without the exercise of contact. Our data shows that, whatever may or may not be the advantages of contact from the point of view of behavioural adjustment, it is certainly a major factor in the likelihood that financial support will be provided by the "outside" parent.

When the courts say, as they frequently do, that it is better for a child to be brought up by its natural parents than by strangers in blood,[6] the judges cite no evidence to support this general assertion. It would be difficult to find clear evidence that this is so. Studies comparing the adjustment of adopted with non-adopted children produce varied results.[7] But for truly valid

---

[6] *Re K. (a minor) (wardship: adoption)* [1991] 1 FLR 57; *Re O.* [1992] 1 FLR 77; *Re W.* [1993] 2 FLR 625. Compare also *Re M.* [1996] 2 FCR 473 with *J. v. C.* [1970] AC 668.

[7] See Seglow *et al* (1972) (good adjustment of adopted children by age 7); Raynor (1977) (70 per cent of 109 adoptees found to be making excellent life adjustment); Tizard (1977) (children adopted from institutional care fared better intellectually and emotionally than children "restored" from care to their natural parents; Triseliotis (1989). Brodzinsky *et al* (1987) review American findings showing higher incidences of difficulties among adopted children.

comparisons to be made it would be necessary to eliminate the many variable factors which might affect the comparison, such as the children's experiences before the adoption, or the way they learn about the adoption, and then compare adopted and non-adopted children who are brought up in comparable circumstances by equally "good" parents. So the claim that "it is better for a child" to be brought up by natural parents is better understood as a claim that "it is better *that*" a child should be so brought up, in the sense that such upbringing better reflects social evaluations of the proper way in which parent-child relationships should be structured. The presumption in favour of contact with an "outside" parent can be seen to be of a similar nature. It encapsulates the viewpoint that it would be wrong to deny children the opportunity to develop a relationship they might possibly value and also wrong to deny the same opportunity to a parent who wanted it.

If the presumption in favour of contact expresses, at least partly, a right of the child, does it follow that a parent is under a duty to provide it? Our evidence shows that the exercise of contact is related to the time the parent in question had lived with the child before separating. In other words, it is an extension of an existing social parenthood. We might assume that parents act as if there is a *social* obligation to sustain and develop social parenthood when it is strongly established even though it can no longer be exercised in one household. The law of Scotland, however, goes further and imposes a *legal* obligation on a parent who is not living with the child "to maintain personal relations and direct contact with the child on a regular basis", enforceable at the suit of the child.[8] This is, however, confined to married parents,[9] though the Scottish Law Commission had recommended that the duty should apply to all parents.[10] The exclusion of non-married parents approximates the provision quite closely to the apparent social rules suggested by our evidence. But the more profound question is whether social parenthood can be created by legal obligation. We doubt it. Our evidence showing how strongly the strand of parental responsibility comprised in the support obligation is resisted when the liable parent is not acting as the social parent of the child in question (and especially if he is at the same time the social parent of another child), suggests that any attempt to enforce "personal relations" by legal means is unlikely to succeed. It is necessary to be cautious about the capacity of legal obligations to overcome strong, countervailing social obligations. The better strategy is to build on existing social obligations, which in this case means encouraging the initial establishment and sustaining of social parenthood.

---

[8] Children (Scotland) Act 1995, s. 1(1)(c).
[9] *Ibid.* s. 3(1)(b).
[10] Scottish Law Commission (1992: 14).

"Social" and "natural" parenthood

The competition between two conceptions of parenthood, the social and the "natural", is at the very heart of this study. We observed in Chapter 3 how policy has vacillated between grounding familial obligations on the social fact of the household and the biological fact of parenthood, and that the Child Support Act 1991 for the most part devalued the obligations which social parenthood might create. This study indicates that the "social" dimension of parenthood plays a far more important part in the performance of the parental role (and therefore probably in the perception of parental obligations) than the policy underscoring the Child Support Act allowed. This is seen in the following major findings: *first*, the strong association between the maintenance of contact with and support by the "outside" parent and the age of the child at separation; *secondly*, the strong negative effect which the presence or subsequent acquisition of a partner by either parent had on the maintenance of contact with and support by the "outside" parent of children with whom they had not lived, or with whom they had lived only for a relatively short time; and *thirdly*, the strong association between the payment of support and the exercise of contact.

However, the attitudinal survey showed that there was a strong gender factor lying behind people's perceptions of their cross-household support obligations. The fathers related their obligations much more closely to the exercise of social parenthood both by themselves and by another man who may have joined the mother's household than the mothers would have allowed. In view of such a division, we should perhaps not speak of *a* social rule, but of *two conflicting* social rules. The empirical data strongly showed the fathers acting consistently with the viewpoints they expressed in the attitudinal survey. They can be said to assume a social rule which can be formulated in three stages: (i) a prior social parenthood developed in a household can be extended beyond that household after parental separation; (ii) social parenthood so extended can create a social obligation to provide support; and (iii) such social obligations can co-exist with the social obligations associated with subsequently acquired social parenthood. Since each stage is dependent on the preceding stage for its existence, *if an initial social parenthood had not existed, or, if it had existed, if it was not extended after separation*, the men will be reluctant to view any support obligation based solely on their natural fatherhood as co-existing with subsequent social parenthood and will be inclined to assume that the obligation attaches to a man who later takes on social parenthood with respect to their child.

The implications of this finding for parental support obligations are complex. It could not be right to conclude that fathers like those already partnered fathers in the "never-together" group should have no support obligations towards the children they have procreated simply because they have not lived with them. It also seems dangerous to say that only those fathers who have looked after their children should have continuing obligations towards them, for this seems to punish virtue. Furthermore, the mothers saw that natural fatherhood, at least when initiated in marriage, created in itself a strong support obligation and were less likely than the fathers to see this as lapsing if the child acquired a stepfather. It is not surprising that mothers should place more weight on natural parenthood and fathers more weight on social parenthood because, for almost all mothers, but by no means all fathers, natural parenthood and social parenthood coincide.

This division can be bridged only if social parenthood were to follow from all instances of natural parenthood. The presumption in favour of contact might be justified on this ground alone. From a practical point of view, investment in social assistance and venues such as "contact centres" could assist the process. The data showed that, even in the case of the fathers in the "never-together" group, who exercised social parenthood less than the fathers in any other group, a significant minority kept in frequent touch with the mother and baby in the period immediately after the birth. However, success in this strategy will always be incomplete. The law therefore imposes a support obligation on fathers solely on the basis of their natural parenthood, unsupported by social parenthood. As we have said, this could hardly be otherwise, lest a penalty be placed on social parenthood. Here the legal obligation diverges from the social obligation (at least, as perceived by the fathers). The reason is that its basis is different. A support obligation which accompanies or arises from social parenthood is embedded in that social parenthood; thus the payment of support can be seen as part of the relationship maintained by continued contact. But an obligation based on natural parenthood rests on the policy of instilling a sense of responsibility for individual action and equity between fathers who do and fathers who do not exercise social parenthood.

But we also saw that fathers considered that the support obligation should be modified by the obligations accompanying a subsequent social parenthood, whereas mothers did not. The Child Support Act 1991 followed the mothers' standpoint. We have explored earlier how family law can be viewed as a field of interaction between legal and social rules. One of the difficulties which has confronted the implementation of the Act has arisen from the conflict between the legal support obligation, based on natural parenthood, and the social obligation towards their new household-families perceived by fathers to arise out of social parenthood. Whether the legal obligation can easily prevail over the social is a matter of observation. Since our research was carried out in the first year in which the Act was in operation, we cannot present any evidence on the matter. However, the difficulties encountered by the Child Support Agency have been a matter of common knowledge, and many of the adjustments made subsequent to its introduction have been concessions in favour of the competing social obligations.

It is as yet not possible to evaluate whether the total net income achieved by the scheme (given the costs of administration) relative to social security spending on one-parent families is any more successful than that revealed by the Finer Committee in 1974 (see p. 43). Nevertheless, Marsh, Ford and Finlayson's (1997) report on the impact of the scheme *on lone parents* during its first eighteen months indicated that although the *proportion* of lone parents who had previously been receiving maintenance payments had not risen,[11] the *amounts* of maintenance actually paid to those who did receive it increased from £32 to £39 a week (average) and from £20 to £25 a week (median).[12] Seven out of ten lone parents with court orders thought they were too low, compared to only a quarter of those with CSA assessments, though 18 per cent thought the CSA assessments were too high. About half who received maintenance under an agreement "of some kind" thought it was too low. Hence the scheme has had a measurable effect on the incomes of some lone parents. The researchers claimed that, for those who were in low-paid work and receiving Family Credit, who can keep £15 of the maintenance payment (the rest going to offset the Family Credit payment), the combination of earnings, Family Credit and maintenance creates enhanced work incentives and opportunities.

Where the assessment was *not* paid, 84 per cent of lone parents in the study were on Income Support and 9 per cent on Family Credit,[13] illustrating the high proportion of cases dealt with by the Agency where the caregiving parent is receiving state support. Where a CSA assessment was paid, the researchers found that the lone parent was in receipt of Income Support in 66 per cent of cases, on Family Credit in 17 per cent, and on neither in another 17 per cent. So in 34 per cent of cases where payment was made, it represented real money to the lone parent. Although the researchers calculated that, of all child maintenance paid to lone parents, only half goes to the state, the rest being retained by the caregiving parent, the Agency itself stated that in the first six months of 1996 it collected £112 million, of which only £48 million was passed on to the parent with care.[14] But another £70 million was paid directly from "outside" parents to caregiving parents as a result of Agency intervention.

A smaller study found no benefits to lone parents as a result of CSA intervention, and that some parents were worse off because intervention led to a cessation of informal help from the "outside" parent, or the loss of benefits associated with Income Support.[15] Even the larger study had found that

---

[11] Marsh, Ford and Finlayson (1997: 69). The reasons for this were the CSA assessments were made on those who were paying or would have paid anyway, or that they were made on those who were not required to pay, or, if so required, would not have paid anyway and still do not pay.

[12] Although there was some reduction since 1995 due to the modifications of the Child Support Act 1995 (see p. 42).

[13] Marsh, Ford and Finlayson (1997: Table 5.5).

[14] Child Support Agency, *Mid-Year Report 1996/7*.

[15] Clarke, Craig and Glendinning (1996).

within its first eighteen months, the scheme had not increased the proportion of outside parents who paid child maintenance, though it observed that that might change as enforcement improved because where the circumstances of the non-payer were known to the lone parent, "the majority were said to be in full-time jobs".[16] Our own findings, which were not of course confined to lone parents, are more pessimistic in this regard (see p. 129), especially with respect to formerly married fathers, though we did find that 14 per cent of the formerly cohabiting fathers who paid nothing, and 21 per cent of the "never-together" fathers who paid nothing, were known to be in full-time work and to be living on their own.

The Agency continues to suffer from administrative delay and enforcement problems. The administration of the scheme remains unduly complex, particularly in the calculation of housing costs, which form part of the liable parents' exempt income.[17] By October 1996, assessments had attained only 77 per cent accuracy.[18] In 1996/7 only 25 per cent of payments required to be paid through the Agency were complied with fully. Partial compliance was achieved in 34 per cent of such cases, though compliance with payments made directly to the caregiving parent is higher, giving a total full compliance achievement of 54 per cent and partial compliance of 21 per cent.[19]

Our previous research[20] had concluded that maintenance payments could enhance work incentives by boosting the incomes of recipients who were in low-paid work, and it is probable that the scheme has improved these incentives still further. But the extent to which it has "saved" public expenditure overall is unclear. Its limited success regarding both compliance and coverage reflects the fact that the scheme straddles the normative divide between mothers and fathers, and the tension between natural and social parenthood, revealed in this study. In recent years there has been a tendency to emphasize the biological basis of familial relationships. It can be strongly argued that an individual's biological origins may be an important aspect of that individual's sense of self-identity. There is therefore a growing appreciation that people may have a right to information about their natural origins, and this right can create a social or legal obligation on others to make this available.[21] But the extent to which natural relationships generate obligations may be perceived to be relatively limited. Obligations which are embedded in social parenthood may be more extensive and more durable.

---

[16] Marsh, Ford and Finlayson (1997: xvii).
[17] See *Annual Report of the Chief Child Support Officer 1995–96* (Department of Social Security, 1996).
[18] Bennett (1997: 7).
[19] Child Support Agency, *Mid-Year Report 1996/7*.
[20] Eekelaar and Maclean (1986).
[21] See Wilson (1997).

Methodological Appendix

THE NEED FOR EMPIRICAL WORK

Chapter 2 described how the social context within which family obligations are located is changing with the emergence of new patterns of family formation and dissolution, resulting in more complex and fluid family structures. Children may be born to parents who live together and are married, who live together without any legal relationship as partners (though the father may register his parental responsibility for a child), or to parents who have never lived together and whose relationships span the range from those who may have no contact to those who may have an ongoing or even a close relationship.

Standard data sets taking a snapshot picture can tell us how many children are born within marriage, how many outside marriage to parents who register the birth together, thereby implying a parental relationship even if not necessarily a co-resident partnership, and how many to a mother who registers the birth in her name only. They can also tell us about current lone parent families, whether they are headed by the mother or the father, and how the lone parental status originated. But it is not easy from data sets like the *General Household Survey* and the Census to see how the child's experience of parenting changed over time, particularly if the parents' relationships change in ways not directly regulated by the law. For example, if they cohabit and then separate, there is no public event to record which would make the changed situation visible to the researcher . Nor is it possible from standard data sets to identify the changing pathways of these children through experience of new partnerships formed by the parent they live with or the parent who lives elsewhere, or their relationships with the new children who may be brought into or born into these new partnerships. In order to throw light on our research about the nature of the parental obligation, both how it is perceived and acted upon by parents and how it is regulated by the law throughout childhood, we found it necessary therefore to carry out an empirical study of what may be termed cross household parenting.

We wished to look beyond the categorisation imposed by legal and visible events such as marriage and divorce, and to locate people across a broader range of family structures in which children are not living with both their biological parents. It was not effective to use any existing sampling frame. The Child Benefit records, for example, which would include those households receiving lone parent benefit, would have excluded children living with a stepparent, and divorce records would have excluded separated unmarried couples. We therefore decided to use a national survey organisation to carry out a screening survey to identify all the kinds of parents we wished to include.

The screening question we chose was "Are you the natural or adoptive parent of a child under 18 whose other parent lives elsewhere?" The interviewer would then prompt: " This includes children living with EITHER parent". This question mirrors the identifying query used by the Child Support Agency to identify cases where a financial obligation from an absent parent to the household of the parent with care should be assessed. It identifies mothers and fathers who have never lived together, who may have lived together or married and then separated or divorced, those living with the child and those living elsewhere, and those who may now be living with or be married to a partner who is not the other parent of the child chosen for our study. After the screening survey had identified all the parents in whom we were interested, they were then asked to agree to take part in a second longer and more detailed interview, to be carried out by Social and Community Planning Research (SCPR) at a later date.

RESEARCH DESIGN

To be eligible for the survey, respondents needed to be the natural or adoptive parent of a child under 18 and living apart from the other parent of the child. We would include therefore not only lone parents but also parents who had repartnered since separating from the other parent of the child.

Screening survey

The sample of parents was screened from a large continuous omnibus survey carried out by a major market research organisation. That survey covers a random sample of adults aged 18 or over in England, Scotland and Wales, and interviews 2,000 adults per week.

Screening questions were piloted by the market research organisation and found to provide up to 100 eligible parents from one week of fieldwork. It was therefore agreed that the screening question would be incorporated in the organisation's questionnaire for six weeks in order to provide the addresses of at least 500 eligible parents .

The screening questions asked were:

"i) Are you the natural or adoptive parent of a child whose other parent lives elsewhere?

Interviewer prompt: This covers children living with either parent.

If yes

ii) In the future, a more detailed survey on the profile of the modern family is going to take place across Britain. This survey will be conducted by another company who specialise in research on social issues and they would be very interested in your views on these matters. The company conducting the research is called SCPR, which stands for Social Community Planning Research and they would like to contact you in the future to ask you some questions on modern family life today. Would you be willing to participate in this survey in the future?"

Sample achieved

Following the screening survey we decided for the time being to concentrate on the respondents from England and Wales, and this reduced the numbers available for the second stage slightly. We also experienced a difficulty with the screening question, in that as the market research organisation question-naire had at several earlier points defined a child as aged under 18, the organ-isation felt that it would be annoyingly repetitive to the respondent to repeat this definition. We therefore omitted it, with the result that a number of peo-ple reported to us children who turned out on recall to be over 18. As a result of this, SCPR interviewers were instructed to establish eligibility at the start of the recall interview. The six weeks of screening yielded a total of 540 usable addresses. Unfortunately, 184 were found to be ineligible by the interviewers on recall. The majority of these (112) had children over 18. There were also other reasons for ineligibility: forty-eight had misunderstood the question or been recorded wrongly as they were not in fact separated and nine had no children. Four cases had been correctly coded, but had reconciled before the second interview and were no longer separated. There were eleven other inel-igible cases. Among the 356 eligibles, there were 106 others with whom it was not possible to cary out a successful interview: fourteen people had moved and could not be traced, forty-one could not be traced, thirty-two refused to take part in the second interview, and nineteen were ill or away or broke the appointment made for other reasons. Thus 249 of the 356 eligible names were successfully interviewed, i.e. 70% of the addresses issued. If we were to assume a similar rate of ineligibility among those not successfully contacted, then the response rate would rise to 76%.

Differences between age groups and gender in the sample

In a population screening exercise we might expect to identify equal numbers of separated mothers and fathers. However fewer men than women were identified as eligible for this survey (65% of the contacted sample were women, 35% were men). There are a number of possible reasons for this.

First, there is a general trend in general population surveys for low response rates among young men. Therefore it is likely that the age range of the men interviewed by the market research organisation as part of the original continuous survey was skewed towards the older age groups. In the sample passed to SCPR, 45% of the men were aged 45 and older, compared with only 22% of the women. Of the sample identified by the initial screening exercise, more men than women were confirmed on contact by the SCPR interviewers to be ineligible (56% of the men compared with 31% of the women). Given that the male sample was already skewed towards the older age group, this led to a high proportion of the male sample being ineligible on the grounds of the age of the child. Another factor which may well have had a bearing on the unequal distribution of men and women in the sample is the fact that some of the men interviewed in the screening survey may have been unaware that they were in fact fathers.

Development of the questionnaire for the recall interview

The second recall or in depth interviews were designed to investigate the life course of a particular child. Thus, the questionnaire structure was such that once an eligible child had been selected, (randomly if more than one eligible child was reported by one respondent) the questions covered events in the respondent's life since the birth of that child including job changes, income level and sources, house moves, new partners and children and so on. At each event in the child's life, questions were designed to check the impact of those events on the relationship of the child with both parents and on the arrangements for the financial support of the child. The interviewers used two separate questionnaires: a household questionnaire and an individual questionnaire. The household questionnaire covered the following topics: (i) who was currently living in the household, (ii) details of the respondent's children both those living with him or her and those living elsewhere, and (iii) any children of the respondent's current partner, again both those living in the household and those living elsewhere.

There were two versions of the individual questionnaire. Questionnaire One (coloured yellow) was for respondents who had lived together, either as married or cohabiting partners, since the child was born. The second questionnaire (coloured green) was for those respondents who had never cohabited with the other parent during the child's lifetime.

The individual questionnaire was divided into eight sections, covering where the child lived at the time of the interview and how much contact there was with the other parent, where the child had lived before and after the separation, the main source of income and level of income of the family before and after separation, the work status of both parents when the child was born and at the time of separation and at the time of interview, parental employment, qualifications, relationships, maintenance arrangements (including any contact with the Child Support Agency), both what was arranged and what payments were actually made. Thus we hoped to able to trace the child's parenting experience in terms of their standard of living and their relationships with both of their parents and any new partners or children of either parent. As the household structures in which these children and their absent parents lived changed over time, we hoped to be able to record the changes in parental behviour and to look for factors which might be associated with them.

Finally we asked about attitudes to child support. Attitudinal survey research is notoriously difficult to undertake with any acceptable degree of validity or reliability. But it is generally held (see Genn and Maclean (1979)) that the closer the matter is to the experience of the respondent and the closer the question is to a preference choice, the higher will be the level of reliability.

In this study we are relatively confident of the reliability of the replies given as we were talking to people with direct experience of cross household parenting who had therefore considered these matters. In addition we had designed our questions in the form of short scenarios or vignettes, about which we asked questions in the form of preference choices while also giving the respondents the opportunity to talk more freely about the reasons for their choices. These verbatim responses were listed and postcoded. The vignettes were designed to explore the attitudes of our sample of people with experience of cross-household parenting to the priorities to be given to conflicting calls on the resources of a parent living outside the child's household.

The questionnaire was piloted in April 1994 by three experienced interviewers, who reported that respondents were enthusiastic and willing to cooperate. The only difficulty lay in the length of the interview. We therefore omitted some of the detailed question about job description and about the absent parent, and went into the field in June 1994. Interviewing was completed by the end of August 1994.

Respondent status in achieved sample

The sample covered both custodial (78% of our total sample of 249 parents) and non-custodial parents (22% of our total sample). The majority of the parents living with their children were women (94%). The majority of parents living apart from their children were men (91%).

Among the sample of men, twelve out of sixty-one (19%) were cases in which the man had custody of the child. (There were a small number of additional cases where the man did not have custody of the study child but the children of the partnership were divided between the parents and the father had custody of other children). Among the sample of women, only five out of 188 (3%) were cases in which the custodial parent was the father. Thus the

Table A1: Proportion of Men and Women as Custodial or Non-custodial Parents

	Custodial parent	Non-custodial parent	Total
Men	12 (6%)	49 (91%)	61 (25%)
Women	183 (94%)	5 (9%)	188 (73%)
Total	195 (100%)	55 (100%)	50 (100%)

sample of men appears to be biased towards custodial fathers. This may be because the pervading atmosphere at the time of the survey was one of suspicion towards the Child Support Agency, and non-custodial men may have been more wary of taking part in a survey about maintenance for fear of a CSA investigation. The disproportionate number of custodial men in the sample may also be in part due to the fact that a number of men separated from their ex-partners either may not be aware that they are fathers, or may not be willing to discuss the matter.

The data therefore must be regarded as possibly biased by under representation of fathers, particularly non-custodial fathers.

The data was processed by SCPR and analysed using SPSS for Windows at the Oxford Centre with the aid of Sarah Beinart of SCPR and Dymphna Hermanns, research associate of the Centre.

Given the small numbers per cell in parts of the analysis, percentages are not always used, and are always rounded. In order to examine the relative effect on our continuing contact variable, we used a logistic regression and calculated chi-squared significance tests on a number of two-way tables. The numbers were too small for the former analysis to yield definitive results. But when looking for factors associated more often than could be the result of chance we found that, if we looked at the data for all those who had lived together with their child, that those who remained in contact were significantly more likely to be the parents of children who were over 5 at the time of separation, and that there was less likelihood that a new partner would be involved with either parent. But if we separate out the parents who had been married from those who had lived together unmarried, we found that the the age of the child at separation has more impact among the married than among the cohabitants, who tended to separate when children were younger, and that the impact of a new partner was more marked among the cohabitants, whose post-separation link with the child appears to be more vulnerable than among the married parents.

Bibliography

AMATO, P. R. and KEITH, B. (1991), "Parental divorce and adult well-being: a meta-analysis", 53 *Journal of Marriage and the Family* 45

ANDERSON, M. (1983), "What is new about the modern family: an historical perspective?" in OPCS Occasional Paper 31, *The Family*

—— (1988), "Households, families and individuals: some preliminary results from the national sample from the 1851 census of Great Britain", *Continuity and Change*, vol. 3, 432

ARMITAGE, B. and BABB, P. (1996), "Population Review: (4) Trends in Fertility", *Population Trends*, No. 84, (Summer) 7

BAINHAM, A. (1993), *Children: the Modern Law* (Bristol, Family Law/Jordan Publishing)

BARTON, C. and DOUGLAS, G. (1995), *Law and Parenthood* (London, Butterworths)

BENNETT, F. (1997), *Child Support: Issues for the Future* (London, Child Poverty Action Group)

BLACK, D. (1989), *Sociological Justice* (Oxford, Oxford University Press)

BLACKSTONE, Sir W. (1775), *Commentaries on the Laws of England*, Book 1, 7th edn (Oxford, Clarendon Press)

BLOCK, J. H., BLOCK, J. and GJERDE, P. F. (1986), "The Personality of Children Prior to Divorce: A Prospective Study", 57 *Child Development* 827

BOWLBY, J. (1951), *Maternal Care and Mental Health* (Geneva, World Health Organisation)

—— (1969), *Attachment and Loss: Attachment* (London, Hogarth Press)

BRADSHAW, J. and MILLAR, J. (1991), *Lone Parent Families in the UK*, DSS Research Report No. 6 (HMSO)

BRADSHAW, J. (1996), *Lone Mothers and Work* (London, Joseph Rowntree Foundation, Findings No. 96)

BRODZINSKY, D. M., RADICE, C., HUFFMAN, L. and MERKLEY, K. (1987), "Prevalence of Clinically Significant Symptomatology in a Nonclinical Sample of Adopted and Nonadopted Children", 16 *Journal of Clinical Child Psychology* 350

BROPHY, J. (1982), "Parental Rights and Children's Welfare: some problems of strategy in the 1920s", 10 *International Journal of the Sociology of Law* 149

BUCHANAN, C. M., MACCOBY, E. E. and DORNBUSCH, S. N. (1991), "Caught between Parents: Adolescents' Experience in Divorced Homes", 62 *Child Development* 1008

BUCHANAN, C. M., MACCOBY, E. E. and DORNBUSCH, S. N. (1996), *Adolescents after Divorce* (Cambridge, Mass., Harvard University Press)

BURGHES, L. with BROWN, M. (1995), *Single lone mothers: Problems, prospects and policies* (London, Family Policy Studies Centre)

BURGOYNE, J. and CLARK, D. (1984), *Making a go of it: a Study of Stepfamilies in Sheffield* (London, Routledge)

CAMARA, K. and RESNICK, G. (1989), "Styles of Conflict Resolution and co-operation between divorced parents: Effects on Children's Behavior and Adjustment", 59 *American Journal of Orthopsychiatry* 560

CHAMBERS, J. D. (1842), *Jurisdiction of the High Court of Chancery over the Person and Property of Infants* (London, Saunders and Benning)

CHERLIN, A. J. and FURSTENBERG, F. F. (1992), *The American Grandparent* (Cambridge, Mass., Harvard University Press)

CHERLIN, A. J., FURSTENBERG, F. F., CHASE-LANDSDALE, P. L., KIERNAN, K. E., ROBINS, P. K., MORISON, D. R. and TEITLER, J. O. (1992), "Longitudinal studies of effects of divorce on children in Great Britain and the United States", 252 *Science* 1386

CLARKE, A. M. and CLARKE, A. D. B. (1976), *Early Experience: Myth and Evidence* (London, Open Books)

CLARKE, K., CRAIG, G. and GLENDINNING, C. (1996) *Small Change: the Impact of the Child Support Act on Lone Mothers and Children* (London, Family Policy Studies Centre and Joseph Rowntree Foundation)

CLIVE, E. (1980), "Marriage: An Unnecessary Legal Concept?" in J. M. Eekelaar and S. N. Katz (eds), *Marriage and Cohabitation in Contemporary Societies: Areas of Legal, Social and Ethical Change* (Toronto, Butterworths)

COLEMAN, D. and SALT, J. (1992), *The British Population: Patterns, Trends and Processes* (Oxford, Oxford University Press)

COLEMAN, J. (1990), *Foundations of Social Theory* (Cambridge, Mass, Harvard University Press)

CROWTHER, M. A. (1982), "Family Responsibility and State Responsbility in Britain before the Welfare State", *Historical Journal*, vol. 25, 131

DENCH, G. (1996), *Exploring Variations in Men's Family Roles* (London, Joseph Rowntree Foundation, Findings No. 99)

DEWAR, J. (1992), *Law and the Family* (London, Butterworths)

EEKELAAR, J. (1973), "What are Parental Rights?", 89 *Law Quarterly Review* 210

—— (1976), "Public Law and Private Rights: the Finer Proposals", *Public Law* 64

—— (1979), "Some Principles of Financial and Property Adustment on Divorce", 95 *Law Quarterly Review* 253

—— (1984), *Family Law and Social Policy*, 2nd edn (London, Weidenfeld & Nicolson)

—— (1991), "Are Parents Morally obliged to care for their Children?", 11 *Oxford Journal of Legal Studies* 340

—— (1991b), *Regulating Divorce* (Oxford, Oxford University Press)

—— (1996), *A Survey of Post-Divorce Financial and Property Adjustment*, Report to the Law Commission

—— (1997), "Child Support: Judial or Computerized Justice?" in T. Oldham (ed), *Child Support: the Next Frontier* (forthcoming)

EEKELAAR, J. and CLIVE, E. (1977), *Custody after Divorce* (Oxford, Centre for Socio-Legal Studies)

EEKELAAR, J. and MACLEAN, M. (1984), "Financial provision on divorce: a reapparaisal" in Michael D.A. Freeman (ed), *State, Law, and the Family: Critical Perspectives* (London, Tavistock Publications and Sweet & Maxwell)

—— (1986), *Maintenance after Divorce* (Oxford, Oxford University Press)

—— (1988), "The Evolution of Private Law Maintenance Obligations: the Common Law" in Marie-Thérèse Meulders-Klein and John Eekelaar (eds), *Family, State and Individual Economic Security* (Brussels, Story Scientia)

—— (1994), *A Reader on Family Law* (Oxford, Oxford University Press)

ELLIOTT, B. J. and RICHARDS, M. P. M. (1991), "Children and Divorce: Educational Performance and Behaviour before and after Parental Separation", 5 *International Journal of Law & the Family* 258

EMERY, R. E. (1994), *Renegotiating Family Relationships: Divorce, Child Custody and Mediation* (New York, The Guilford Press)

ERMISCH, J., DI SALVO, P. and JOSHI, H. (1996), *Household Formation and housing tenure decisions of young people* (University of Essex, ESRC Research Centre on Micro-Social Change)

FERRI, E. (1984), *Stepchildren: A National Study* (Windsor, Nfer-Nelson)

FINCH, J. (1989), *Family Obligations and Social Change* (Cambridge, Polity Press)

FINER, Sir M. and MCGREGOR, O. R., "A History of the Obligation to Maintain", App. 5 of *Report of the Committee on One-Parent Families*, vol. 2, (Cmnd. 5629-I) (London, HMSO, 1974)

FUNDER, K. and SMYTH, B. (1996), *Family Law Evaluation Project 1996: Parental Responsibilities: Two national surveys (Part One: Report)* (Melbourne, Australian Institute of Family Studies)

FURSTENBERG, F. F. and SPANIER, S. (1984), *Recycling the Family* (New York, Sage)

FURSTENBERG, F. F., MORGAN, S. and ALLISON, P. (1987), "Paternal participation and children's well-being after marital dissolution", 52 *American Sociological Review* 695

FURSTENBERG, F. and CHERLIN, A. (1991), *Divided Families: What happens to children when parents part* (Cambridge, Mass, Harvard University Press)

GENERAL HOUSEHOLD SURVEY 1994 (London, HMSO, 1996)

GENN, H. and MACLEAN, M. (1979), *Methodological Issues in Social Surveys* (London, Macmillan)

GIBSON, C. (1994), *Dissolving Wedlock* (London, Routledge)

——— (1996), "Contemporary Divorce and Changing Family Patters" in M. Freeman (ed) *Divorce: Where Next?* (Aldershot, Dartmouth)

GLENDON, M. A. (1976), "Marriage and the State: the Withering Away of Marriage", 62 *Virginia Law Review* 663

——— (1989), *The Transformation of Family Law: State, Law, and Family in the United States and Western Europe* (Chicago, University of Chicago Press)

GOLDSTEIN, J., FREUD, A. and SOLNIT, A. J. (1973) *Before the Best Interests of the Child* (New York, The Free Press)

GRAY, K. (1977), *The Reallocation of Property on Divorce* (Abingdon, Professional Books)

HART, H. L. A. (1994), *The Concept of Law*, 2nd edn (Oxford, Oxford University Press)

HASKEY, J. (1987), "One-person households in Great Britain: living alone in the middle years of life", *Population Trends*, No. 50, (Winter), 23

——— (1989), "Trends in marriage and divorce, and cohort analyses of the proportions of marriages ending in divorce", *Population Trends*, No. 54, 21

——— (1993), "Trends in the numbers of non-parent families in Great Britain", *Population Trends*, No. 71, 26

——— (1994), "Estimated numbers of one-parent families and their prevalence in Great Britain in 1991", *Population Trends*, No. 78, (Winter), 5

——— (1994b), "Stepfamilies and stepchildren in Great Britain", *Population Trends*, No. 76, 17

HASKEY, J. (1995), "Trends in marriage and cohabitation: the decline in marriage and the changing pattern of living in partnerships", *Population Trends* No. 80, (Summer), 5

—— (1996), "The proportion of married couples who divorce: past patterns and current prospects", *Population Trends* No. 83 (Spring) 25

—— (1996b), "Divorce and children: fact proven and interval between petition and decree", *Population Trends*, No. 84 (Summer) 28

—— (1996c), "Population Review: (6) Families and Households in Great Britain", *Population Trends* No. 85 (Autumn) 7

HEALY, J. M., MALLEY, J. E. and STEWART, A. J. (1990), "Children and their Fathers after Parental Separation", 60 *American Journal of Orthopsychiatry* 531

HESS, R. D. and CAMARA, K. A. (1979), "Post-divorce relationships as mediating factors in the consequences of divorce for children", 35 *Journal of Social Issues* 79

HESTER, M. and RADFORD, L. (1996), *Domestic Violence and Child Contact in England and Denmark* (Bristol, Policy Press, University of Bristol)

HETHERINGTON, E. M. (1989), "Coping with marital transitions: winners, losers and survivors", 60 *Child Development* 1

HOGGETT, B. (1980), "Ends and Means: the Utility of Marriage as a Legal Institution", in J. M. Eekelaar and S. N. Katz (eds), *Marriage and Cohabitation in Contemporary Societies: Areas of Legal, Social and Ethical Change* (Toronto, Butterworths)

HONORÉ, T. (1993), "The Dependence of Morality on Law", 13 *Oxford Journal of Legal Studies* 1

JOHNSTON, J. KLINE, M. and TSCHANN, J. T. (1989), "Ongoing postdivorce conflict: effects on children of joint custody and frequent access", 59 *American Journal of Orthopsychiatry* 576

KIERNAN, K. and ESTAUGH, V. (1993), *Cohabitation: Extra-marital childbearing and social policy* (London, Family Policy Studies Centre)

KIERNAN, K. and WICKS, M. (1990), *Family Change and Future Policy* (London, Family Policy Studies Centre)

KIERNAN, K. (1996), "Lone Motherhood, Employment and Outcomes for Children", 10 *International Journal of Law, Policy & the Family* 233

KLINE, M., JOHNSTON, J. and TSCHANN, J. M. (1991), "The long shadow of marital conflict: a model of children's postdivorce adjustment", 53 *Journal of Marriage and the Family* 297

KRAUSE, H. D. (1976), "Creation of Relationships of Kindred" in A. G. Chloros (ed), *International Encyclopedia of Comparative Law* (Tubingen, J.C.B. Mohr, Paul Steinbeck)

LAND, H. (1995), "The Crumbling Bridges between Childhood and Adulthood" in J. Brannen and M. O'Brien (eds), *Children in Families: Research and Policy* (Falmer Press)

LASLETT, P. (1983), *The World we have lost—further explored*, 3rd edn (London, Methuen)

Law Commission (1969), *Family Law: Report on Financial Provision in Matrimonial Proceedings*, Law Com No 25 (London, HMSO)

—— (1979), *Family Law: Illegitimacy*, Working Paper No. 74 (London, HMSO)

—— (1982), *Family Law: Illegitimacy*, Law Com No 118 (London, HMSO)

LONG, N., FOREHAND, R., FAUBER, R. and BRODY, G. H. (1987), "Self-perceived and independently observed competence of young adolescents as a function of parental marital conflict and recent divorce", 15 *Journal of Abnormal Child Psychology* 15

LONG, N., SLATER, E., FOREHAND, R. and FAUBER, R. (1988), "Continued High and Reduced Parental Conflict following Divorce in Relation to Young Adolescent Adjustment", 56 *Journal of Consulting and Clinical Psychology* 467

LOWE, N. V. (1997), "The Meaning and Allocation of Parental Responsibility", 11 *International Journal of Law, Policy & the Family*, 192

MACFARLANE, A. (1986), *Marriage and Love in England 1300–1840* (Oxford, Blackwell)

MACCOBY, E. E. and MNOOKIN, R. H. (1992), *Dividing the Child: Social and Legal Dilemmas of Custody* (Cambridge, Mass, Harvard University Press)

MACLEAN, M. and EEKELAAR, J. (1993), "Child Support: the British Solution", *International Journal of Law & the Family* 205

MACLEAN, M. and WADSWORTH, M. E. J. (1988), "The Interests of Children after Parental Divorce: a long-term perspective", 2 *International Journal of Law & the Family* 155

MACLEAN, M. and WARMAN, A. (1997), "A Comparative Approach to Child Support Systems: Legal Rules and Social Policies", in T. Oldham (ed), *Child Support: the Next Frontier* (forthcoming)

MAIDMENT, S. (1984), *Child Custody and Divorce* (Beckenham, Croom Helm)

MARSH, A., FORD, R. and FINLAYSON, L. (1997), *Lone Parents, Work and Benefits*, Department of Social Security Research Report No. 61 (London, The Stationery Office)

MCGREGOR, O. R., BLOM-COOPER, L. and GIBSON, C. (1970), *Separated Spouses* (London, Duckworth)

MCLANAHAN, S. and SANDEFUR, G. (1994), *Growing up with a Single Parent: what helps, what hurts* (Cambridge, Mass, Harvard University Press)

MCRAE, S. (1993), *Cohabiting Mothers: Changing Marriage or Motherhood?* (London, Policy Studies Institute)

MILLAR, J. and WARMAN, A. (1996), *Family Obligations in Europe* (School of Social Sciences, University of Bath, mimeo)

MORROW, V. and RICHARDS, M. (1996), *Transitions to Adulthood: A family matter?* (London, Joseph Rowntree)

MURPHY, M. (1995), "Are Cohabiting Unions More Likely to Break Down Than Marriages?", *Changing Britain* (London, ESRC)

OGUS, A., BARENDT, E. and WIKELEY, N. J. (1995), *The Law of Social Security*, 4th edn, (London, Butterworths)

PEART, N. (1996), "Towards a Concept of Family Property in New Zealand", 10 *International Journal of Law, Policy & the Family* 105

PRIEST, J. A. and WHYBROW, J. C (1986), *Custody Law in Practice in the Divorce and Domestic Courts*, Supplement to Law Commission Working Paper No. 96 (London, HMSO)

PRYOR, J. and SEYMOUR, F. (1996), "Making decisions about children after parental separation", 8 *Child and Family Law Quarterly* 229

RAYNOR, L. (1977), "Twenty-one plus and adopted", 87 *Adoption and Fostering* 38

RAZ, J. (1996), "On the Nature of Law", 82 *Archiv fur Rechts- und Sozialphilosophie* 1

RICHARDS, M. P. M. (1987), "Children, Parents and Families: Developmental Psychology and the Re-orientation of Relationships at Divorce", 1 *International Journal of Law & the Family* 295

———— (1994), "Divorcing Children: Roles for Parents and the State" in M. Maclean and J. Kurczewski (eds), *Families, Politics and the Law*, (Oxford, Clarendon Press)

RUNCIMAN, W. G. (1983) *A Treatise on Social Theory*, vol. 1 (Cambridge, Cambridge University Press)

RUTTER, M. (1972), *Maternal Deprivation Reassessed* (Harmondsworth, Penguin Books)

Scottish Law Commission (1992), *Report on Family Law*, Scot. Law Com No 135 (London, HMSO)

SEGLOW, J., KELLMER-PRINGLE M. L. and WEDGE, P. (1972), *Growing up Adopted* (Windsor, National Foundation for Educational Research)

SIMPSON, A. H. (1875), *A Treatise on the Law and Practice relating to Infants* (London, Stevens and Haynes)

SMART, C. (1989), "Power and the Politics of Custody" in C. Smart and S. Sevenhuijsen (eds), *Child Custody and the Politics of Gender* (London, Routledge)

SMART, C. and NEELE, B. (1997), "Good enough Morality: Divorce and Postmodernity", *Journal of Law and Society* (forthcoming)

SPRUIJT, E. and DE GOEDE, M. (1996), "Changing Family Structures and Adolescent Well-Being in the Netherlands", 10 *International Journal of Law, Policy & the Family* 1

STRAUSS, P. and STRAUSS, J. (1974), "Review of *Beyond the Best Interests of the Child*", *Columbia Law Review* 1002

TAMANAHA, B. Z. (1995), "An Analytical Map of Social Scientific Approaches to the Concept of Law", 15 *Oxford Journal of Legal Studies* 501

THÉRY, I. (1993), *Le Démariage* (Paris, Editions Odile Jacob)

THOMSON, D. (1986), "Welfare and the Historians" in L. Bonfield et al (eds), *The World we have Gained* (Oxford, Oxford University Press)

—— (1989), "The Elderly in an Urban-Industrial Society: England 1750 to the Present" in J. Eekelaar and D. Pearl (eds), *An Aging World: Dilemmas and Challenges for Law and Social Policy* (Oxford, Oxford University Press)

TIZARD, B. (1977), *Adoption: A second chance* (London, Open Books)

TRISELIOTIS, J. (1989), "Foster-care outcomes: a review of key research findings"

UTTING, D. (1995), *Family and parenthood: Supporting families, preventing breakdown* (London, Joseph Rowntree Foundation)

WALLERSTEIN, J. S. and KELLY, J. B. (1980), *Surviving the Breakup: How Children and Parents cope with Divorce* (London, Grant McIntyre)

WALLERSTEIN, J. S. and BLAKESLEE, S. (1989),*Second Chances: Men, Women & Children a Decade After Divorce* (London, Bantam Press)

WARDLE, L. D. (1993), "The Evolving Rights and Duties of Stepparents: Making New Rules for New Families", in J. Eekelaar and P. Sarcevic (eds), *Parenthood in Modern Society: Legal and Social Issues for the Twenty-First Century* (Dordrecht, Martinus Nijhoff)

WIERSON, M., FOREHAND, R. and McCOMBS, A. (1988), "The relationship of early adolescent functioning to parent-reported and adolescent-perceived interparental conflict", 16 *Journal of Abnormal Child Psychology* 707

WILSON, G. (1987), "Money: Patterns of Responsibility and Irresponsibility in Marriage", ch. 7 in J. Brannen and G. Wilson (eds), *Give and Take in Families* (London, Allen & Unwin)

WILSON, S. (1997), "Donor Insemination and Identity" 11 *International Journal of Law, Policy & the Family* 270

Table of Statutes

Table of Cases

Index